Great Meals in Minutes was created by Rebus, Inc. and published by Time-Life Books.

Rebus, Inc.

Publisher: Rodney Friedman
Editorial Director: Shirley Tomkievicz

Editor: Marya Dalrymple
Art Director: Ronald Gross
Managing Editor: Brenda Goldberg
Senior Editor: Charles Blackwell
Food Editor and Food Stylist: Grace Young
Photographer: Steven Mays
Prop Stylist: Cathryn Schwing
Staff Writer: Alexandra Greeley
Associate Editor: Bonnie J. Slotnick
Editorial Assistant: Ned Miller
Assistant Food Stylist: Karen Hatt
Photography Assistant: Edward Santalone
Recipe Tester: Gina Palombi Barclay
Production Assistant: Lorna Bieber

For information about any Time-Life book, please write:
Reader Information
Time-Life Books
541 North Fairbanks Court
Chicago, Illinois 60611

Library of Congress Cataloging in Publication Data
Family menus.
   (Great meals in minutes)
   Includes index.
   1. Cookery, American.   2. Menus.
I. Time-Life Books. II. Series.
TX715.F1943   1985   642′.1   85-8496
ISBN 0-86706-290-8 (lib. bdg.)
ISBN 0-86706-289-4 (retail ed.)

First printing. Printed in U.S.A.
Published simultaneously in Canada.
School and library distribution by Silver Burdett Company, Morristown, New Jersey.
TIME-LIFE is a trademark of Time Incorporated U.S.A.

Time-Life Books Inc. is a wholly owned subsidiary of

Time Incorporated

Founder: Henry R. Luce 1898–1967
Editor-in-Chief: Henry Anatole Grunwald
President: J. Richard Munro
Chairman of the Board: Ralph P. Davidson
Corporate Editor: Jason McManus
Group Vice President, Books: Reginald K. Brack Jr.
Vice President, Books: George Artandi

Time-Life Books Inc.

Editor: George Constable
Executive Editor: George Daniels
Editorial General Manager: Neal Goff
Director of Design: Louis Klein
Editorial Board: Dale M. Brown, Roberta Conlan, Ellen Phillips, Gerry Schremp, Gerald Simons, Rosalind Stubenberg, Kit van Tulleken, Henry Woodhead
Director of Research: Phyllis K. Wise
Director of Photography: John Conrad Weiser

President: William J. Henry
Senior Vice President: Christopher T. Linen
Vice Presidents: Stephen L. Bair, Robert A. Ellis, John M. Fahey Jr., Juanita T. James, James L. Mercer, Joanne A. Pello, Paul R. Stewart, Christian Strasser

Editorial Operations
Design: Ellen Robling (assistant director)
Copy Room: Diane Ullius
Editorial Operations: Caroline A. Boubin (manager)
Production: Celia Beattie
Quality Control: James J. Cox (director), Sally Collins
Library: Louise D. Forstall

SERIES CONSULTANT
Margaret E. Happel is the author of *Ladies' Home Journal Adventures in Cooking*, *Ladies' Home Journal Handbook of Holiday Cuisine*, and other best-selling cookbooks, as well as the translator and adapter of Rebecca Hsu Hiu Min's *Delights of Chinese Cooking*. A food consultant based in New York City, she has been director of the food department of *Good Housekeeping* and editor of *American Home* magazine.

WINE CONSULTANT
Tom Maresca combines a full-time career teaching English literature with writing about and consuming fine wines. He is the author of *Mastering Wine a Taste at a Time*.

Cover: Dorothee Polson's Sloppy Joes with oven fried potatoes and garnishes. See pages 96–97.

Great Meals
IN MINUTES

FAMILY
MENUS

TIME-LIFE BOOKS, ALEXANDRIA, VIRGINIA

Contents

MEET THE COOKS 4

FAMILY MENUS IN MINUTES 7

PANTRY 14

EQUIPMENT 16

Meet the Cooks

DIANA STURGIS

Welsh by birth and now living in Brooklyn with her family, Diana Sturgis graduated from the University of Wales in Cardiff with a teaching diploma. She taught cooking and nutrition for eight years before moving to the United States. Her background includes recipe development and testing for a New York food company and freelance food styling. At present, she is director of the test kitchen at *Food & Wine* magazine.

ANN BURCKHARDT

Born and educated in Iowa, Ann Burckhardt began her food career on the editorial staff of the Betty Crocker Cookbooks at General Mills. She is the author of *Writing about Food and Families, Fashion and Furnishings*, and is currently the editor of "Taste," the Wednesday food section of the *Minneapolis Star & Tribune*.

LUCY WING

A native of Arizona, who now lives in New York City, Lucy Wing worked as a home economist in the Best Foods Division of CPC International Inc. She has been contributing editor for *Country Living* magazine and is currently food editor of *McCall's*. Her articles have appeared in *Family Circle, SELF*, and *Cuisine*.

JANE KIRBY

Jane Kirby is a registered dietitian who has worked in various capacities during her food career: as a hospital staff dietitian; a freelance public relations consultant; an assistant food editor for *Good Housekeeping* magazine; and a test kitchen coordinator for *Ladies' Home Journal*. Since 1979, she has been the food editor of *Glamour* magazine.

NINA SIMONDS

Nina Simonds learned to cook in the Far East under the direction of Chinese master chefs and under the tutelage of Chinese cooking authority Huang Su Huei. She also studied for a year at L'Ecole de Cuisine La Varenne in Paris. She is a regular contributor to the *Boston Globe* food pages, and has written for *Gourmet, Cuisine, The Pleasures of Cooking*, and the *Washington Post*. She is the author of *Classic Chinese Cuisine*.

MARIANNE LANGAN

Home economist and food stylist Marianne Langan's food career began in the test kitchens of the Campbell Soup Company. She then moved to Standard Brands, where she supervised all of the food photography. Since 1984, she has worked as a freelance cookbook writer and as a stylist for many major food companies and magazines.

LONI KUHN

Born and raised on a large cattle ranch in northern California, Loni Kuhn now lives and works in San Francisco. She was food editor of *San Francisco Magazine* and currently teaches part-time in her own cooking school, Cook's Tours. She is also a restaurant consultant and part owner of a company specializing in California food products.

KATHLEEN KENNY SANDERSON

Kathleen Kenny Sanderson, who lives in New York, is a graduate of the California Culinary Academy in San Francisco. She cooked at L'Escargot in San Francisco, and later was personal chef for the Robert Kennedy family. Besides teaching cooking at the New School for Social Research in New York City, she also works as a freelance food consultant.

DOROTHEE POLSON

Phoenix resident Dorothee Polson, an eleven-time winner of the Vesta Award for newspaper food writing and editing, was the food editor for twenty-three years for the *Arizona Republic* and now writes a weekly food column for that paper. She is the author of *Dorothee Polson's Pot au Feu Cookbook*, which includes recipes as well as a number of her columns on the vagaries of family life.

Family Menus in Minutes

GREAT MEALS FOR FOUR IN AN HOUR OR LESS

As American food writer M.F.K. Fisher remarks in her *Alphabet for Gourmets,* "F is for family...and the depths and heights of gastronomical enjoyment to be found at the family board." For better or worse, what we learn at the family table shapes our attitudes about food and eating. And it is there, too, that we learn about manners and morals, the value of good conversation—and life.

Traditions of the family table endure—passed on from generation to generation. What, when, and how we eat says more about who we are and where we come from than about hunger. The chocolate chip cookies we ate as snacks are still our favorite because they suggest the comfort of home. What Mom served at Thanksgiving is probably what *we* offer our guests on that holiday. If we grew up in the South eating fried chicken with cream gravy and spoonbread, chances are we dream fondly of these dishes—even prepare them—though we now live in California.

Despite our nostalgia for good home cooking and all it entails, today's fast-paced lifestyle more often than not prevents the whole family from sitting down to eat at the same time. Work, fast-food restaurants, and television have taken their toll on the family meal.

On the following pages, nine of America's most talented cooks present 27 complete family menus especially created for busy parents. These simple, budget-wise recipes provide a delicious, nutritious alternative to convenience foods and are all designed to lure every family member back to the table. Some of the dishes are standard family favorites—pigs in blankets and meat loaf—while others introduce more unusual fare. There are recipes for Italian, Mexican, French, and Chinese dishes—along with some American regional offerings—many of which can be served hot or cold, and for lunch as well as for dinner.

Each menu, which serves four people, can be prepared in an hour or less, and the cooks focus on foods from the basic food groups—dairy, vegetables/fruit, meat/fish/poultry, and bread/grains—that growing children require. Every recipe uses fresh produce, with no powdered sauces or other dubious shortcuts. The other ingredients called for (vinegars, spices, herbs, and so on) are all of high quality and are usually available in supermarkets.

When planning family meals, consider some of these easy, guaranteed-to-please dishes: coleslaw, corn wheels, hot popovers, sausage and cheese pizza, turkey, pepper, and mushroom kabobs, and pigs in blankets.

The cooks and the kitchen staff have meticulously planned and tested the menus for appearance as well as for taste, as the accompanying photographs show: The vegetables are brilliant and fresh, the visual combinations appetizing. The table settings feature bright colors, simple flower arrangements, and attractive but not necessarily expensive serving dishes.

In addition, the Editors, with advice from the cooks, give suggestions for the use of leftovers, and for complementary side dishes and desserts. On each menu page, you will also find a number of tips, from an easy method for stuffing bell peppers to advice for selecting the freshest produce.

BEFORE YOU START

Great Meals in Minutes is designed for efficiency and ease. This book will work best for you if you follow these suggestions:

1. Refresh your memory with the few simple cooking techniques on the following pages. They will quickly become second nature, and you will produce professional-quality meals in minutes.

2. Read the menus before you shop. Each lists the ingredients you will need, in the order that you would expect to shop for them. Many items will already be on your pantry shelf.

3. Check the equipment list on page 16. Good sharp knives and pots and pans of the right shape and material are essential for making great meals in minutes. This may be the time to buy a few things: The right equipment can turn cooking from a necessity into a creative experience.

4. Set out everything you need before you start to cook. The lists at the beginning of each menu tell just what is required. To save effort, always keep your ingredients in the same place so you can reach for them instinctively.

5. Follow the start-to-finish steps for each menu. That way, you can be sure of having the entire meal ready to serve in an hour.

WHAT'S FOR DINNER?

With the wide variety of fresh ingredients available in the markets today, deciding what to serve the family for dinner is easier than ever before. Still, all parents face some challenges at the dinner table: How to teach children sound eating habits. How to teach them that eating well not only satisfies hunger but also is essential to good health. There are no easy solutions, but the following tips may help.

Cooking at high temperatures will be less dangerous if you follow a few simple tips:

▶ Water added to hot fat will always cause spattering. If possible, pat foods dry with a cloth or paper towel before you add them to the hot oil.

▶ Place food gently into any pan containing hot fat, or the fat will spatter.

▶ If you are boiling or steaming some foods while sautéing others, place the pots on the stove top far enough apart so that the water is unlikely to splash into the hot fat.

▶ Turn pot handles inward, so that you do not accidentally knock over a pot containing hot foods or liquids.

▶ Remember that alcohol—wine, brandy, or spirits—may occasionally catch fire when you add it to a very hot pan. If this happens, step back for your own protection and quickly cover the pan with a lid. The fire will instantly subside, and the food will not be spoiled.

▶ Keep pot holders and mitts close enough to be handy while cooking, but *never* hang them over the burners or lay them on the stove top.

By offering a wide assortment of foods from the basic food groups, parents can be assured that their children are getting the nutrients they need. By the age of six or seven, most children are willing to experiment with new tastes, and many begin to accept foods they once spurned—particularly if parents are enthusiastic about them. Many of the recipes in this volume contain foods your children may never have had. Now is a good time to introduce them into their diet.

Wise and practical parents take advantage of their children's natural curiosity and tendency to imitate, and use the market, the kitchen, and the family table as teaching tools. Once children are involved in the selection and preparation of food, they will inevitably begin to learn the lessons of good eating.

At the Market

Take children to the supermarket and let them read to you the shopping lists and labels on the packages. As you select foods, explain the seasonality of fruits and vegetables, and describe the difference between white and whole-wheat flours, or regular and skimmed milk, for example. Explain why certain foods are more healthful than others. Send older children to gather certain items from the supermarket shelves. When checking out, try to avoid the candy displays, and once home, encourage your children to help you stock the kitchen cupboards.

In the Kitchen

Many of the menus in this volume include recipes that are easy enough for children to help prepare. Give them their own bright, washable aprons, and provide them with shelf space for some pots, pans, and other kitchen equipment that you provide solely for their own use. Look over the recipes together before beginning, and have all ingredients within easy reach. While the food is cooking, ask the children to set the table—perhaps referring to the photographs in this volume for guidance—and later to help you serve the dinner.

At the Table

Children delight in sunny colors and tantalizing textures, so be sure to incorporate them into your meals, in both the food and the table setting. Don't be afraid to reintroduce foods in new ways. Keep portions small: Too much food on the plate may intimidate a child or may lead to overeating and weight problems. For children under six, cut food into bite-size pieces for easier handling; they are less likely to refuse it.

Select a tablecloth, napkins, plates, and mugs in lively colors, and utensils that are durable and easy to hold. To eliminate anxiety over spilled food, use an easy-to-clean tablecloth or mats.

Most important, keep mealtimes happy by avoiding disputes. And do not force children to eat. They are the best judges of their appetites and capacity.

Tips on Feeding Teenagers

Teenagers have high daily calorie and nutrient requirements, and those who are very active may need to consume as many as 3,000 calories a day. Unfortunately, as teenagers assert their independence, they are less likely to follow parents' suggestions about wholesome eating, developing instead haphazard habits such as skipping breakfast, following crash diets, and consuming fast-food snacks.

To counter bad eating habits, stock up on high-quality nourishing foods for both mealtimes and snacks. In doing so, keep in mind the particular nutritional needs of teenagers, and carefully select foods rich in calcium, iron, and vitamins B and C. At mealtimes, if weight is not a concern, do not limit portions for teenagers. In fact, you may want to double some of the recipes in this volume, particularly if you are feeding more than one teenager.

And What About You?

Don't let a busy schedule keep you from enjoying meals with the family and from getting proper nutrition yourself. Three meals a day are as essential for parents as they are for children. For snacks, stick to eating the healthful foods you've prepared for the youngsters.

The more hectic your life, the more important it is to plan a week's menus in advance and shop accordingly. Ask the family to tell you what they'd like to eat, take their suggestions into account, and plan meals for variety as well as for nutritional value. Menu planning helps when you don't have the time or energy to be creative. On more relaxed days, shop for the best buys, and purchase what you feel like cooking.

Quick Breads...

Versatile quick breads—made without yeast—live up to their name because they can easily be prepared in less than an hour. In this volume, there are recipes for popovers, scones, Cheddar drop biscuits, cornbread, corn sticks, and sourdough rolls, all of which make excellent accompaniments to a main course. Pancakes, waffles, and certain batter breads are also quick-bread possibilities.

Quick breads are leavened by the action of baking powder or baking soda, and sometimes by steam (as in popovers). Like yeast breads, most quick breads depend upon bubbles of carbon dioxide gas for their lightness.

For assured success when making quick breads, follow these simple rules:

1. Handle the dough or batter as little as possible. With most quick breads, mix just until the dry ingredients are moistened, even if some lumps remain. Overbeating produces a bread with a coarse, tough texture. When using baking powder or soda as the sole leavening agent, always mix it with the dry ingredients before adding the liquids.

2. Bake the bread immediately after mixing, otherwise too much carbon dioxide escapes and the bread will not rise properly.

3. Never overbake quick breads or they will dry out and form hard crusts. To test for doneness with loaves, muffins, and biscuits, insert a toothpick or skewer into the center; if it comes out clean, the bread is done. Properly baked loaves will have a rounded top that may appear slightly cracked; this is normal.

Serve muffins or biscuits hot or cool. Loaves should be cooled completely for easier slicing. Popovers should be served piping hot (you can reheat them), and pancakes and waffles may be served hot or cold.

Popovers, which Ann Burckhardt prepares in her Menu 1, page 31, are delicious served for breakfast and lunch as well as dinner. Split and filled, they make a delicious light meal with soup or salad. Offer your family some of these popover variations:

Tuna melt: Mix your favorite tuna salad combination and spoon it into popover halves. Top with sliced tomato and shredded cheese, and bake in a 400-degree oven for 3 to 4 minutes, or until the cheese melts.

Monte Cristo: Layer slices of ham, chicken, and tomato in popover halves, then place a slice of Swiss or Cheddar cheese on top of each half. Bake popovers in a 400-degree oven for 3 to 4 minutes, or until the cheese melts.

Chili popovers: Ladle chili into hot popover halves, then top with grated Cheddar cheese, sour cream, minced scallions, and diced avocado. Serve immediately.

...and Pizza Dough

Yeast dough for pizza can be quickly made in a food processor, as Diana Sturgis shows in her Menu 1 on page 21. However, making pizza dough the traditional way—by hand—can be a fun activity for the whole family when there is time.

Evelyne Slomon's Pizza Dough by Hand

1 cup hot tap water
1 package active dry yeast
3½ cups all-purpose white flour, approximately
½ teaspoon salt
Vegetable oil for greasing bowl

1. In medium-size mixing bowl, combine hot water with yeast, stirring gently with fork until yeast has dissolved and liquid turns light beige.

2. Add 1 cup flour and salt, and stir with a wooden spoon to combine. Add another cup of flour and mix until dough starts to pull away from sides of bowl and begins to form a soft, sticky mass.

3. Sprinkle some flour over work surface and flour your hands generously. Remove dough from bowl and knead in another cup of flour, one-quarter cup at a time.

4. With heel of one hand (or both hands, if you wish), push dough across floured work surface. Grab dough with one hand and twist and fold it over. Scrape up any moist dough that sticks to work surface. Working quickly, repeat this action, adding only as much of remaining flour as it takes to keep dough from sticking to your hands.

5. To test, push the heel of your hand into dough for 10 seconds. If your hand comes up clean, the dough is ready; if it is sticky, a bit more kneading will be necessary. Be careful not to overwork the dough; continue kneading only until it is smooth and elastic, about 5 to 10 minutes.

6. Clean the bowl and lightly grease it with vegetable oil. Place dough in bowl and turn dough until evenly coated with a thin film of oil. Cover bowl securely with plastic wrap.

7. Let dough rise 30 to 45 minutes in a warm, draft-free place, preferably in a gas oven with a pilot light or in an electric oven preheated to 200 degrees and then turned off.

8. Once dough has doubled in bulk, punch it down with your fist, turn it onto a lightly floured surface, and knead it for another minute.

Advance Preparation of Pizza Dough

Refrigerated rising: To prepare pizza dough a day ahead, follow the recipe above through step 6, and refrigerate dough. The next morning, punch dough down and knead it for 1 minute. Return dough to bowl, cover, and refrigerate. Be sure to remove dough from refrigerator at least 30 minutes before rolling it out.

Freezing: After step 6 above, flatten dough into ½-inch-thick disk, wrap in plastic, and freeze. Defrost dough for 24 hours in a refrigerator, or set it in a warm place (at least 80 degrees) for 2 hours. Use the dough as soon as it is warm enough to handle. Although the dough will not double in bulk, follow step 8.

FAMILY BEVERAGES

No family meal is complete without a beverage that complements the food and suits the season. Because many parents prefer not to drink wine or other alcoholic beverages when children are at the table, for this volume the Editors have not provided specific drink suggestions with each menu. However, the following tips should guide you in selecting appropriate beverages for the entire family.

For sound nutrition, avoid serving soft drinks at meals. Plain milk or milk-based drinks, fruit juices, sparkling, tap, or mineral water, or hot or iced herb teas are much better mealtime choices. Since children are far more sensitive to caffeine than adults, avoid serving them beverages containing caffeine, if possible.

Milk Drinks

Milk—whole, skimmed, low-fat, or buttermilk—with its supply of protein, calcium, phosphorus, riboflavin, and vitamin D, is a valuable food for most children and many adults. Because of its neutral flavor, milk is wonderfully versatile and combines well with a number of flavorings (such as syrups and purées) and enrichments (such as eggs and yogurt). The following recipes for milk-based drinks are particularly enjoyable with a family meal. An enriched milk drink, accompanied by a few crackers or some granola, makes a particularly good on-the-go breakfast. If you prefer, use low-fat or skimmed milk, and decrease the amount of sweetener. Each recipe yields one serving, but the quantities can be increased proportionally.

Eggnog shake: In the container of a blender, combine 1 cup chilled milk, 1 whole egg, 1 teaspoon honey, 1 teaspoon vanilla extract, and a pinch of nutmeg, and blend until frothy.

Chocolate-peanut butter shake: In the container of a blender, combine ¾ cup milk, 2 tablespoons chocolate syrup, and 2 tablespoons peanut or other nut butter. Blend until frothy.

Rich hot cocoa: In medium-size heavy-gauge saucepan, combine ½ cup milk and ½ cup light cream and heat over low heat. Meanwhile, combine 1 tablespoon cocoa and 1 tablespoon sugar in a small bowl. When the milk is hot, slowly pour it into the cocoa-sugar mixture, stirring to combine. Add ½ teaspoon vanilla and pour the liquid back into the saucepan to heat through before serving.

Yogurt-banana frappe: In the container of a blender, combine 1 cup milk, ½ ripe banana cut into chunks, ½ cup plain yogurt, 1½ teaspoons honey, 1 teaspoon vanilla extract, and ½ teaspoon lemon extract, and blend until frothy.

Juices

Busy cooks often resort to serving canned apple or tomato juice at mealtime, but freshly prepared fruit and vegetable juices are more refreshing, flavorful, and often more nutritious than their canned or packaged counterparts.

Take advantage of whatever produce is in season, selecting the ripest fruits or vegetables for maximum juice content. Wash all produce thoroughly in cold water, then cut out bruised areas, stem, pits, or seeds. To get the most juice, have fruits or vegetables at room temperature. Store fresh juices in tightly covered containers in the refrigerator, and serve them as soon as possible.

The following drinks made from freshly prepared fruit or vegetable juices are good with meals or as a snack. Each of these recipes yields one serving, but the quantities can be increased proportionally.

Fresh pineapple juice: Select a ripe pineapple. Trim and discard ends. Cut pineapple lengthwise into quarters, then remove rind and core. Cut fruit into cubes, drop the cubes into the container of a blender or food processor, and process until smooth. Strain the purée, if desired, and serve it over ice. Sweeten if desired.

Citrus cooler: Combine 1 cup freshly squeezed orange juice, 2 tablespoons lemon juice, ¼ cup soda water, and pour over ice cubes. Garnish with a sprig of mint and serve.

Frozen fruit ices: Pour your children's favorite freshly squeezed fruit juice into small paper cups, then place the cups in the freezer. When the juice begins to harden, insert a popsicle stick into each cup. When completely frozen, peel off the paper and serve like ice pops.

Vegetable thirst quencher: Combine 1 cup fresh tomato juice, ½ medium-size cucumber, peeled, seeded, and chopped, 2 tablespoons chopped parsley, and ⅓ cup chopped celery in the container of a blender or food processor, and process until smooth. Add salt, pepper, and lemon juice to taste. Serve over ice.

Drinks for Adults Only

For those who like wine or beer with a meal, the menus in this volume are particularly well suited to domestic beers or ales and many inexpensive wines, including jug wines. Domestic wines are particularly recommended.

When buying domestic wines, Americans are often confused by the sheer diversity of choices available to them. Keep in mind that domestic wines are divided into three basic categories: proprietary, generic, and varietal. All three types offer good value, especially proprietary wines from the West Coast.

Proprietary wines are so called because they are named and trademarked by the proprietor of a vineyard. Often these wines are simply named "Red Table Wine" or "California White," but sometimes they are given wildly fanciful appellations. Because proprietary wines are exempt from federal regulation, a vintner can experiment by combining different types of grapes into a single wine. Often prized grape varieties are used, resulting in some splendid proprietary wines. Since these wines are blends and differ greatly in quality and taste, it is impossible to generalize about them. Therefore, when you purchase a proprietary wine, base your choice upon the reputation of the winery, not on the name of the wine.

Generic wines, a peculiarly American invention, are domestic wines that bear the names of European wines or wine regions, even though they may not taste like their European counterparts. Many jug wines, such as California Chablis and Burgundy, fall into this class.

Healthy Snacks

Most children need to nibble between meals because they burn up so much energy. Therefore, the quality of the snacks they eat is important: Snacks should be wholesome foods rather than empty-caloried sweets such as soft drinks and candy bars. The following suggestions are good for youngsters—and adults, too:

Cheeses: Hard and semisoft cheeses such as Cheddar, Jarlsberg, and Muenster are good sources of protein and calcium. Cut into wedges, strips, or cubes, and wrapped in plastic bags in individual 2-ounce portions, these cheeses make a handy and nutritious snack—especially when accompanied by fresh fruit and some whole-grain bread. If your children particularly love cheese, you should probably serve them relatively low-fat types such as cottage cheese, farmer cheese, or skim-milk ricotta and mozzarella.

Cereals: Delicious not only for breakfast, cooked or cold whole-grain cereals with fruit and milk are also splendid energy boosters between meals, offering protein, carbohydrates, vitamins, minerals, and fiber. Many families enjoy granola cereal, a combination of various grains, nuts, and sweeteners that varies from brand to brand. Beware, however: Many commercial granolas are loaded with oil, sugar, and salt. To be sure the granola you eat has the highest food value, make your own. (See the recipe that follows.)

Nuts and seeds: Nuts and seeds, as well as peanuts (which are legumes), are excellent sources of protein, complex carbohydrates, vitamins E, B1 and B12, and minerals. Commercial processing can destroy the nutritive value of these foods, so your best bet is to choose raw or "natural" nuts and seeds, usually available at health food stores. For a better value, buy them in the shell. You can easily make a tasty snack by combining lightly toasted nuts, seeds, and dried fruit. (See the recipe that follows.)

Fruits: Fresh seasonal fruits, good sources of vitamins (especially vitamin C) and minerals, are excellent snacks: They are sweet, portable, and low enough in calories that seconds do not have to be forbidden. Do not overlook dried fruits—apricots, dates, raisins, and figs—which are particularly high in iron.

Available year round but at their peak in the fall, apples are an especially good snack. In fact, some dentists claim that apples are almost as good for the teeth as a toothbrush.

Some apples are best cooked; others are more suitable for eating raw. Look for apples that are firm and well colored, and do not buy any with blemishes or soft spots. Smaller apples are usually a better buy than larger ones. To prolong storage, do not wash apples before storing them, and handle them gently to avoid bruising them. Wrapped in plastic bags and stored in the refrigerator or in a cool place, crisp, firm apples should keep about two weeks.

Some of the most popular eating varieties include:

Cortland: Two-toned red and yellow, with snowy white, somewhat tart flesh. Bruise resistant.

Delicious: Usually large and juicy in both the Red and Golden varieties. Generally sweet and flavorful, but tasteless if they've been stored too long.

Granny Smith: Crisp, tart, lime-green; available year round.

McIntosh: Red-green, aromatic, crisp, tart-sweet.

Low-fat yogurt: This creamy, cultured milk product is packed with protein and calcium. Plain, low-fat yogurt, an almost perfect food on its own, can be made more palatable for children by the addition of cut-up fresh fruit, such as bananas, berries, or peaches. Sweetened yogurt and yogurt products (made from whole milk) are relatively high in calories and undesirable as snacks.

Homemade Granola

Making granola is simple—just moisten raw grains and nuts with water, add oil and flavorings, and toast until the moisture evaporates.

½ cup coarsely chopped dates
½ cup raisins
2 cups rolled oats
2 cups rolled wheat
1 cup sesame seeds
½ cup chopped unsalted nuts, such as unblanched almonds
1 cup whole-wheat flour
¼ cup safflower oil
¼ cup honey
2 tablespoons ground cinnamon
1 tablespoon vanilla extract

1. Preheat oven to 250 degrees.
2. Place dates and raisins separately in two small bowls, add enough warm water to cover, and set aside to soak at least 15 minutes, or until soft.
3. Combine rolled oats and wheat, sesame seeds, nuts, and whole-wheat flour in large bowl. Add 1 cup water, oil, honey, cinnamon, and vanilla, and stir until moistened.
4. Spread mixture out on large baking sheet and toast, stirring frequently with metal spatula, about 30 minutes, or until steam no longer rises from pan.
5. Meanwhile, drain raisins and dates, and dry.
6. Remove toasted ingredients from oven. Add raisins and dates to pan, stir to combine, and toast another 3 to 4 minutes.
7. Remove granola from oven and set aside to cool completely.
8. Turn mixture into plastic bag or covered container and store in refrigerator. Serve with milk or yogurt, as a topping for fruit, or simply as an out-of-hand snack.

Fruit-Nut Snack

½ pound unblanched almonds
½ pound unsalted cashews
2 teaspoons salt (optional)
1 cup hulled sunflower seeds
½ cup raisins
1 cup hulled pumpkin seeds
½ cup chopped dates

1. Preheat oven to 250 degrees.
2. Arrange nuts on baking sheet in a single layer and sprinkle with salt, if desired. Toast nuts in oven, shaking pan frequently, 10 to 15 minutes, or until nuts are golden.
3. Remove nuts from oven and set aside to cool.
4. Combine nuts and remaining ingredients in a large bowl and toss until evenly distributed.
5. Turn mixture into tightly covered container and store in a cool place.

Making Stock

Although canned chicken broth or stock is all right for emergencies, homemade chicken stock has a rich flavor that is hard to match. Moreover, the commercial broths—particularly the canned ones—are likely to be oversalted.

To make your own stock, save chicken parts as they accumulate and put them in a bag in the freezer; then have a rainy-day stock-making session, using the recipe below. The skin from a yellow onion will add color; the optional veal bone will add extra flavor and richness to the stock.

Basic Chicken Stock

3 pounds bony chicken parts, such as wings, back, and neck
1 veal knuckle (optional)
3 quarts cold water
1 yellow unpeeled onion, stuck with 2 cloves
2 stalks celery with leaves, cut in two
12 crushed peppercorns
2 carrots, scraped and cut into 2-inch lengths
4 sprigs parsley
1 bay leaf
1 tablespoon fresh thyme, or 1 teaspoon dried
Salt (optional)

1. Wash chicken parts and veal knuckle (if you are using it) and drain. Place in large soup kettle or stockpot (any big pot) with the remaining ingredients—except salt. Cover pot and bring to a boil over medium heat.
2. Lower heat and simmer stock, partly covered, 2 to 3 hours. Skim foam and scum from top of stock several times. Add salt to taste after stock has cooked 1 hour.
3. Strain stock through fine sieve placed over large bowl. Discard solids. Let stock cool uncovered (this will speed cooling process). When completely cool, refrigerate. Fat will rise and congeal conveniently at top. You may skim it off and discard it or leave it as a protective covering until ready to use.

Yield: About 10 cups.

Beef stock, although time-consuming to make, requires very little attention while cooking. Use marrow bones and an inexpensive cut of beef, such as shin, in roughly equal amounts. If you use beef knuckle, have the butcher saw it into quarters. During the first few minutes of cooking, the beef and bones will produce a scum that must be carefully removed from the surface, but for the bulk of the cooking time, the stock will require only occasional skimming. The cooking time given is approximate. Long, slow simmering is necessary to extract all the flavor from the ingredients, but a half hour more or less will not matter significantly. When the stock is cooked, leave it uncovered at room temperature until it is completely cool: Stock will turn sour if it is covered while still warm. Stock may be refrigerated for several days or frozen for up to three months.

Beef Stock

1 leek (optional)
2 medium-size carrots
3 to 4 celery stalks with leaves
6 to 8 sprigs fresh parsley
1½ teaspoons chopped fresh thyme or ½ to ¾ teaspoon dried
Large onion
3 cloves garlic (optional)
4 pounds shin of beef with bone
2 pounds marrow bones, or 1 pound marrow bones and 1 beef knuckle
1 bay leaf
6 whole cloves (optional)
8 peppercorns
1½ teaspoons salt

1. Trim and clean leek; peel carrots, wash celery and parsley; chop fresh thyme, if using. Do not peel onion and garlic.
2. Place beef and bones in kettle and add approximately 4 quarts of cold water, to cover beef and bones by about 2 inches. Over moderate heat, bring to a simmer, skimming off scum as it rises.
3. When scum has almost stopped surfacing, add vegetables, herbs, and seasonings and return to a simmer. Partially cover pot and, over low heat, cook stock at a gentle simmer, skimming as necessary, approximately 4 to 5 hours.
4. Taste stock. Cook down further if flavor needs to be intensified, or add water if it has reduced too much and the flavor is too strong.
5. Strain stock through fine sieve into large bowl or jar. Discard bones, meat, vegetables, and seasonings. Allow stock to cool completely, uncovered.
6. Refrigerate stock until a layer of fat has solidified on surface. Remove it with a spoon and discard it. Return defatted stock to refrigerator, or freeze, for future use.

Varietal wines are those named for the grape variety that constitutes between 75 and 100 percent of their contents. Varietals can be among the most expensive American wines, though some of the larger domestic wineries do market inexpensive varietals. Chenin Blanc and Fumé Blanc (white wines) and Zinfandel and Merlot (red wines) are examples of varietals.

GENERAL COOKING TECHNIQUES

Sautéing

Sautéing is a form of quick frying, with no cover on the pan. In French, *sauter* means "to jump," which is what vegetables or small pieces of food do when you shake the sauté pan. The purpose is to brown the food lightly and seal in the juices, sometimes before further cooking. This technique has three critical elements: the right pan, the proper temperature, and dry food.

The sauté pan: A proper sauté pan is 10 to 12 inches in diameter and has 2- to 3-inch straight sides that allow you to turn the food and still keep the fat from spattering. It has a heavy bottom that can be moved back and forth across a burner easily.

The best material (and the most expensive) for a sauté pan is tin-lined copper because it is a superior heat conductor. Heavy-gauge aluminum works well but will discolor acidic foods like tomatoes. Therefore, you should not use aluminum if acidic food is to be cooked for more than 20 minutes after the initial browning. Another option is to select a heavy-duty sauté pan made of strong, heat conducting aluminum alloys. This type of professional cookware is smooth and stick resistant.

Use a sauté pan large enough to hold the food without crowding, or sauté in two batches. The heat of the fat and the air spaces around the pieces facilitate browning.

Many recipes call for sautéing first, then lowering the heat and cooking the food, covered, for an additional 10 to 20 minutes. Be sure to buy a sauté pan with a tight-fitting cover. Make certain the handle is long and is comfortable to hold. Use a wooden spatula or tongs to keep the food moving in the pan as you shake it over the burner. If the food sticks, a metal spatula will loosen it best. Turn the food so that all surfaces come into contact with the hot fat.

Never immerse the hot pan in cold water because this will warp the metal. Allow the pan to cool slightly, then add water and let it sit until you are ready to wash it.

The fat: Half butter and half vegetable or peanut oil is perfect for most sautéing: It heats to high temperatures without burning, yet allows a rich butter flavor. For cooking, unsalted butter tastes best and adds no extra salt.

If you prefer an all-butter flavor, clarify the butter before you begin. This means removing the milky residue, which is the part that scorches. To clarify butter, heat it in a small saucepan over medium heat and, using a cooking spoon, skim off and discard the foam as it rises to the top. Keep skimming until no more foam appears. Pour off the remaining oil—the clarified butter—leaving the milky residue at the bottom of the pan. You may clarify only the amount of butter required for the meal you are preparing, or you may make a large quantity of it and store it in your refrigerator for two to three weeks, if desired.

Some sautéing recipes in this book call for olive oil, which imparts a delicious and distinctive flavor of its own and is less sensitive than butter to high heat. Nevertheless, even the finest olive oil has some residue of fruit pulp, which will occasionally scorch. Watch carefully when you sauté in olive oil; discard any scorched oil and start with fresh, if necessary.

To sauté properly, heat the fat until it is hot but not smoking. When you see small bubbles on top of the fat, lower the heat because the fat is on the verge of smoking. When using butter and oil together, add butter to the hot oil. After the foam from the melting butter subsides, you are ready to sauté. If the temperature of the fat is just right, the food will sizzle when you put it in the pan. Dorothee Polson sautés peppers, page 95.

Stir Frying
This technique requires very little oil, and the foods—which you stir continuously—fry quickly over very high heat. Stir frying is ideal for cooking bite-size, shredded, or thinly sliced portions of vegetables, fish, meat, or poultry, alone or in combination. Kathleen Sanderson stir fries steak and vegetables, page 89.

Blanching
Blanching, or parboiling, is an invaluable technique. Immerse vegetables for a few minutes in boiling water, then refresh them, that is, plunge them into cold water to stop their cooking and set their colors. Blanching softens or tenderizes dense or crisp vegetables, often as a preliminary to further cooking by another method, such as stir frying. Marianne Langan blanches green beans, page 70.

Steaming
Steaming is a fast and nutritious way to cook vegetables and other food. Bring water to a boil in a saucepan. Place the food in a steamer or on a rack over the liquid and cover the pan, periodically checking the water level. Keeping the food above the liquid preserves vitamins and minerals often lost in other methods of cooking. Jane Kirby steams green beans, page 49.

Broiling and Grilling
These are relatively fast ways to cook meat, poultry, and fish, giving the food a crisp exterior while leaving the inside juicy. To add flavor or moisture, brush the food with melted fat, a sauce, or a marinade before and during cooking.

In broiling, the food cooks directly over the heat source. In grilling, the food cooks either directly over an open fire or on a well-seasoned cast-iron or stone griddle placed directly over a burner. Nina Simonds broils turkey kabobs, page 56.

Roasting and Baking
Roasting is a dry-heat process, usually used for large cuts of meat and poultry, that cooks the food by exposing it to heated air in an oven or, perhaps, a covered barbecue. For more even circulation of heat, the food should be placed in a shallow pan or on a rack in a pan. For greater moisture retention, baste the food with its own juices, fat, or a flavorful marinade. Dorothee Polson's Menu 2 features oven-roasted potatoes.

Baking applies to the dry-heat cooking of foods such as casseroles, small cuts of meat, fish, poultry, and vegetables, and, of course, breads and pastries. Some foods are baked tightly covered to retain their juices and flavors; others, such as breads, cakes, and cookies, are baked in open pans to release moisture. Ann Burckhardt bakes popovers, page 31.

Glazing
Glazing foods in their cooking liquid, butter or oil, and a little sugar gives them a slight sheen as the ingredients reduce to a syrupy consistency. Glazing enhances the food's flavor and appearance, and it needs no additional sauce. Nina Simonds glazes carrots in her Menu 2, page 60.

Pan Frying
In pan frying, the food cooks, uncovered, in a small amount of fat that has been preheated in a heavy skillet. This is a quick cooking method, suitable for thin-cut chops, steaks, and other foods. Lucy Wing pan fries potatoes, page 42.

Pantry (for this volume)

A well-stocked, properly organized pantry is essential for preparing great meals in the shortest time possible. Whether your pantry consists of a small refrigerator and two or three shelves over the sink, or a large freezer, refrigerator, and entire room just off the kitchen, you must protect staples from heat and light.

In maintaining your pantry, follow these rules:

1. Store staples by kind and date. Canned goods, canisters, and spices need a separate shelf, or a separate spot on a shelf. Date all staples—shelved, refrigerated, or frozen—by writing the date directly on the package or on a bit of masking tape. Then put the oldest ones in front to be sure you use them first.

2. Store flour, sugar, and other dry ingredients in canisters or jars with tight lids. Glass and clear plastic allow you to see at a glance how much remains.

3. Keep a running grocery list so that you can note when a staple is half gone, and be sure to stock up.

ON THE SHELF:

Baking powder

Baking soda

Chilies, canned
jalapeños
mild green chilies
(Anaheim)

Cornstarch
Less likely to lump than flour, cornstarch is an excellent thickener for sauces. Substitute in the following proportions: 1 tablespoon cornstarch to 2 of flour.

Flour
all-purpose, bleached or unbleached

Garlic
Store in a cool, dry, well-ventilated place. Garlic powder and garlic salt are not adequate substitutes for fresh garlic.

Herbs and spices
The flavor of fresh herbs is much better than that of dried. Fresh herbs should be refrigerated and used as soon as possible. The following herbs are perfectly acceptable dried, but buy in small amounts, store airtight in dry area away from heat and light, and use as quickly as possible. In measuring herbs, remember that one part dried will equal three parts fresh. *Note:* Dried chives and parsley should not be on your shelf, since they have little or no flavor; frozen chives are acceptable. Buy whole spices rather than ground, as they keep their flavor much longer. Grind spices at home and store as directed for herbs.

basil
bay leaves
Cayenne pepper
chili powder
cinnamon
cloves, ground
coriander, whole and ground
curry powder
fennel seeds
mustard
nutmeg, whole and ground
oregano
paprika
pepper
black peppercorns
These are unripe peppercorns dried in their husks. Grind with a pepper mill for each use.
white peppercorns
These are the same as the black variety, but are picked ripe and husked. Use them in pale sauces when black pepper specks would spoil the appearance.
salt
Use coarse salt—commonly available as kosher or sea—for its superior flavor, texture, and purity. Kosher salt and sea salt are less salty than table salt. Substitute in the following proportions: three-quarters teaspoon table salt equals just under one teaspoon kosher or sea salt.
tarragon

thyme

Honey

Hot pepper sauce

Nuts
almonds

Oils
corn, safflower, peanut, or vegetable
Because these neutral-tasting oils have high smoking points, they are good for high-heat sautéing.
olive oil
Sample French, Greek, Spanish, and Italian oils. Olive oil ranges in color from pale yellow to dark green and in taste from mild and delicate to rich and fruity. Different olive oils can be used for different purposes: for example, stronger ones for cooking, lighter ones for salads. The finest quality olive oil is labeled extra-virgin or virgin.

Olives
California pitted black olives
Niçoise, Gaeta, or Kalamata olives

Onions
Store all dry-skinned onions in a cool, dry, well-ventilated place.
red or Italian onions
Zesty tasting and generally eaten raw. The perfect salad onion.
yellow onions
All-purpose cooking onions, strong in taste.

Potatoes, boiling and baking

"New" potatoes are not a particular kind of potato, but any potato that has not been stored.

Rice
long-grain white rice
Slender grains, much longer than they are wide, that become light and fluffy when cooked and are best for general use.

Soy sauce
Extracted from fermented soybeans, both light and dark soy sauces come in a wide range of flavors and brands. The so-called light soy sauce is actually very brown. Japanese-style (not necessarily imported from Japan) soys are probably the best because they are less salty than the Chinese. Dark soy sauces, though actually no browner than the "light," are at once sweeter, saltier, and more concentrated in flavor—very good occasionally but less generally useful than the more common, light variety.

Stock, chicken and beef
For maximum flavor and quality, your own stock is best (see recipe page 12), but canned stock, or broth, is adequate for most recipes and convenient to have on hand.

Sugar
granulated sugar
light brown sugar

Tomatoes
Italian plum tomatoes
Canned plum tomatoes

(preferably imported) are an acceptable substitute for fresh.

tomato paste

tomato sauce

Vinegars

rice vinegar

red and white wine
     vinegars

Wines and spirits

red wine, dry

white wine, dry

Worcestershire sauce

IN THE REFRIGERATOR:

Bread crumbs

You need never buy bread crumbs. To make fresh crumbs, use fresh or day-old bread and process in food processor or blender. For dried, toast bread 30 minutes in preheated 250-degree oven, turning occasionally to prevent slices from browning. Proceed as for fresh. Store bread crumbs in an airtight container: fresh crumbs in the refrigerator and dried crumbs in a cool, dry place. Either type may also be frozen for several weeks if tightly wrapped in a plastic bag.

Butter

Many cooks prefer unsalted butter because of its finer flavor and because it does not burn as easily as salted.

Buttermilk

Celery

Cheese

Cheddar, sharp

A firm cheese, ranging in color from nearly white to yellow. Cheddar is a versatile cooking cheese.

Monterey Jack

From California—a mild

cheese made from skim, partly skim, or whole milk.

mozzarella

A mild cheese, most commonly made from cow's milk. Fresh mozzarella is far superior to packaged and can generally be found in Italian grocery stores.

Parmesan cheese

Avoid the pre-grated packaged variety; it is very expensive and almost flavorless. Buy Parmesan by the quarter- or half-pound wedge and grate as needed: 4 ounces produces about one cup of grated cheese.

ricotta

Made from whey with whole or skim milk added, ricotta resembles cottage cheese but does not separate when cooked.

Swiss

Its sweet, nutlike flavor has made this a popular cheese and it is now made in many countries. The authentic Swiss product has the word "Switzerland" printed on the rind.

Coriander

Also called *cilantro* or Chinese parsley, its pungent leaves resemble flat-leaf parsley. Keep in a glass of water covered with a plastic bag.

Cream

heavy cream

sour cream

Eggs

Will keep 4 to 5 weeks in refrigerator. For best results, bring to room temperature before using, except when separating.

Ketchup

Lemons

In addition to its many uses

in cooking, a slice of lemon rubbed over cut apples and pears will keep them from discoloring. Do not substitute bottled juice or lemon extract.

Limes

Mayonnaise

Milk

Mustards

The recipes in this book usually call for Dijon or coarse-grained mustard.

Parsley

The two most commonly available kinds of parsley are flat-leaf and curly; they can be used interchangeably when necessary. Flat-leaf parsley has a more distinctive flavor and is generally preferred in cooking. Curly parsley wilts less easily and is excellent for garnishing. Store parsley in a glass of water and cover loosely with a plastic bag. It will keep for a week in the refrigerator. Or wash and dry it, and refrigerate in a small plastic bag with a dry paper towel inside to absorb any moisture.

Scallions

Also called green onions. Mild flavor. Use the white bulbs as well as the fresh green tops. Wrap in plastic and store in the refrigerator, or chop coarsely, wrap in plastic, and freeze.

Tortillas, corn

Equipment

Proper cooking equipment makes the work light and is a good cook's most prized possession. You can cook expertly without a store-bought steamer or even a food processor, but basic pans, knives, and a few other items are indispensable. Below are the things you need—and some attractive options—for preparing the menus in this volume.

Pots and pans

Large kettle or stockpot
3 skillets (large, medium, small) with covers; one with oven-proof handle
2 heavy-gauge sauté pans, 10 to 12 inches in diameter, with covers
3 saucepans with covers (1-, 2-, and 4-quart capacities)
  Choose heavy-gauge enameled cast-iron, plain cast-iron, aluminum-clad stainless steel, or aluminum (but you need at least one saucepan that is not aluminum). Best—but very expensive—is tin-lined copper.
Broiler pan with rack
13 x 9 x 2-inch shallow baking pan
17 x 11-inch cookie sheet
12-cup muffin tin
9-inch metal pie pan
Jelly-roll pan
Ovenproof casserole with cover
Ovenproof serving platters
Salad bowl

Knives

A carbon-steel knife takes a sharp edge but tends to rust. You must wash and dry it after each use; otherwise it can blacken foods and counter tops. Good-quality stainless-steel knives, frequently honed, are less trouble and will serve just as well in the home kitchen. Never put a fine knife in the dishwasher. Rinse it, dry it, and put it away—but not loose in a drawer. Knives will stay sharp if they have their own storage rack.
Small paring knife
Bread knife (serrated edge)
10-inch chef's knife
Sharpening steel

Other cooking tools

2 sets of mixing bowls in graduated sizes, one set preferably glass or stainless steel
Flour sifter

Colander with a round base (stainless steel, aluminum, or enamel)
2 sets of measuring cups and spoons in graduated sizes
  One for dry ingredients, another for shortenings and liquids.
Mesh strainer
Slotted spoon
Long-handled wooden spoons
Ladle
Slotted spatula
2 metal spatulas or turners (for lifting hot foods from pans)
Rubber or vinyl spatula (for folding in ingredients)
Rolling pin
Grater (metal, with several sizes of holes)
  A rotary grater is handy for hard cheese.
Small wire whisk
Pair of metal tongs
Wooden board
Garlic press
Vegetable peeler
Vegetable brush
Collapsible vegetable steamer
Mortar and pestle
Pastry brush for basting (a small, new paintbrush that is not nylon serves well)
Cooling rack
Kitchen shears
Kitchen timer
Cheesecloth
Aluminum foil
Paper towels
Plastic wrap
Waxed paper
Kitchen string
Oven mitts or potholders
Small brown paper bag
Thin rubber gloves

Electric appliances

Food processor or blender
  A blender will do most of the work required in this volume, but a food processor will do it more quickly and in larger volume. A food processor should be considered a necessity, not a luxury, for anyone who enjoys cooking.
Electric mixer

Optional cooking tools

Steamer unit
Salad spinner
Butter warmer
Small jar with tight-fitting lid
Spice grinder
Salad servers
Citrus juicer
  Inexpensive glass kind from the dime store will do.
Nutmeg grater
Zester
Deep-fat thermometer
Roll of masking tape or white paper tape for labeling and dating

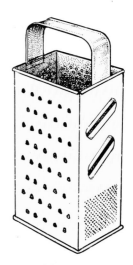

GRATER

COLANDER

STRAINER

FOOD
PROCESSOR

RUBBER
SPATULA

WHISK

METAL
SPATULA

MIXING BOWLS

VEGETABLE PEELER

SHARPENING STEEL

CHEF'S KNIFE

VEGETABLE STEAMER

PARING KNIFE

TONGS

SLOTTED SPATULA

SAUCEPANS

SAUTÉ PAN

SKILLET

Diana Sturgis

D iana Sturgis grew up in a rural area of South Wales where, she says, "fresh foods and sophisticated ingredients were hard to come by." Today, the meals she prepares for her own family are very different from those she ate as a child. She takes advantage of the abundance of fresh produce and imported ingredients widely available in this country, cooking foods that her children already like as well as dishes that are new to the family.

The three menus she offers here are all Italian-style and easy to make. Menu 1 features individual sausage and cheese pizzas, which are preceded by a soup of rice and peas *(risi e bisi)*, slivered ham, and chopped spinach. Orange and kiwi fruit slices are the colorful dessert.

In Menu 2, the stuffed peppers are nearly a meal in themselves, with their rich filling of Italian sausage, bread crumbs, cheese, and pine nuts. Toasted garlic bread and a salad of tomatoes with red onion and fresh basil go well with the peppers.

Diana Sturgis finds that pasta is always a winner at the family table. In Menu 3, she serves a hearty casserole of baked ziti (hollow tubular pasta) with tomato sauce, meatballs, and three types of cheese. Spinach with mushrooms, scallions, and homemade croutons is the simple salad.

For this informal family dinner, offer the soup before the main course of small pizzas topped with tomato sauce, cheese, and a mosaic of sausage slices. The orange and kiwi dessert is enhanced by a dollop of sour cream and a sprinkling of brown sugar.

19

Risi e Bisi Soup
Individual Sausage and Cheese Pizzas
Sliced Oranges and Kiwis

Each single-serving pizza is topped with slices of sweet sausage, a staple of Italian cookery. Italian sweet sausages, available in links at most supermarkets, are usually seasoned with garlic, fennel seeds, and ground black pepper. If you prefer making pizza dough by hand, see page 9.

Kiwi fruit, named for the fuzzy New Zealand bird it resembles, is a rich source of vitamin C. Brown-skinned with lime-green flesh and tiny edible seeds, this tart-sweet fruit is a natural partner for oranges. To ripen hard kiwis, leave them in a closed paper bag with a ripe apple or banana for a couple of days at room temperature. California kiwis are sold from October to May; those imported from New Zealand may be purchased in the summer.

SHOPPING LIST AND STAPLES

2 to 3 sweet Italian sausages (about ½ pound total weight)
2 ounces thinly sliced good-quality baked ham (about 2 or 3 slices)
½ pound fresh spinach, or 10-ounce package frozen chopped spinach
3 navel oranges
3 kiwi fruits
8-ounce container sour cream
8-ounce package mozzarella cheese
10-ounce package frozen tiny green peas
3 cups chicken stock, preferably homemade (see page 12), or canned
8-ounce can tomato sauce
3 tablespoons olive oil
2 tablespoons vegetable oil, approximately
3 cups flour, preferably bread flour or unbleached all-purpose flour, approximately
2 tablespoons yellow cornmeal, approximately
⅓ cup long-grain rice
1 packet (¼ ounce) fast-acting yeast
1 tablespoon granulated sugar
1 tablespoon dark brown sugar
1 teaspoon dried oregano
Salt

UTENSILS

Food processor or blender
Small skillet
Medium-size saucepan with cover
Small saucepan with cover
Four 8- or 9-inch metal pie pans, or two 11 x 17-inch heavy-gauge cookie sheets, or a combination of both
2 medium-size bowls
Small bowl
Large strainer
Measuring cups and spoons
Chef's knife
Paring knife
Wooden spoon
Ladle
Pizza wheel (optional)
Pastry brush
Rolling pin
Grater (if not using processor)

START-TO-FINISH STEPS

1. Follow fruit recipe steps 1 through 4.
2. Follow pizzas recipe step 1 and soup recipe step 1.
3. Follow pizzas recipe steps 2 through 5.
4. While sausages are simmering, follow soup recipe steps 2 through 5.
5. While rice is cooking, follow pizzas recipe steps 6 through 10.
6. Follow soup recipe steps 6 through 9.
7. Follow pizzas recipe steps 11 through 13.
8. While pizzas are baking, follow soup recipe step 10 and serve as first course.
9. Follow pizzas recipe step 14 and serve as main course.
10. Follow fruit recipe step 5 and serve for dessert.

RECIPES

Risi e Bisi Soup

½ pound fresh spinach, or 10-ounce package frozen chopped spinach
⅓ cup long-grain rice
10-ounce package frozen tiny green peas
2 ounces thinly sliced good-quality baked ham (about 2 or 3 slices)
3 cups chicken stock

1. Wash fresh spinach, if using, in several changes of cold water to remove grit. Remove and discard tough stems; set spinach aside.

2. Bring ¼ cup water to a rapid boil in medium-size saucepan over high heat. Add fresh spinach to boiling water, cover pan, and cook 2 minutes.

3. Meanwhile, combine rice with 1 cup of water in small saucepan and bring to a boil over medium-high heat. Reduce heat, cover, and simmer gently 16 to 17 minutes, or just until rice is tender and water is absorbed.

4. Turn spinach into large strainer and drain, pressing with back of spoon to eliminate excess moisture. Coarsely chop spinach; set aside. Rinse pan; set aside. If using frozen spinach, cut package in half with chef's knife or cleaver. Place one half in freezer bag and return to freezer; set remaining half aside. Repeat for frozen peas.

5. Stack ham slices and cut into thin slivers; set aside.

6. When rice is done, remove from heat and fluff with fork; cover pan and set aside.

7. In medium-size saucepan, combine 1½ cups stock, frozen spinach, if using, and peas, and bring to a boil over medium heat. Reduce heat to low and simmer very gently about 4 minutes, or until spinach is thawed and peas are tender.

8. Meanwhile, transfer half the rice to blender or food processor fitted with steel blade. Add remaining 1½ cups stock and process 1 minute, or until puréed.

9. Add puréed rice, remaining boiled rice, slivered ham, and fresh cooked spinach, if using, to stock mixture in saucepan and stir to combine; cover pan and set aside.

10. When ready to serve, reheat soup briefly over medium heat and divide among 4 bowls.

Individual Sausage and Cheese Pizzas

1 packet (¼ ounce) fast-acting yeast
1 tablespoon granulated sugar
2 tablespoons vegetable oil, approximately
3 cups flour, preferably bread flour or unbleached all-
  purpose flour, approximately
1 teaspoon salt
3 tablespoons olive oil
2 to 3 sweet Italian sausages (about ½ pound total
  weight)
8-ounce package mozzarella cheese
2 tablespoons yellow cornmeal, approximately
8-ounce can tomato sauce
1 teaspoon dried oregano

1. For pizza dough, combine yeast and sugar in small bowl. Add 1 cup warm (110 degrees) tap water, stir to combine, and set aside 5 minutes, or until mixture foams.

2. Lightly grease medium-size bowl with vegetable oil; set aside.

3. Combine flour and salt in bowl of food processor fitted with dough blade. With processor running, slowly add 2 tablespoons olive oil, then add yeast mixture. Dough will quickly form a ball on top of blade (this takes 20 to 30 seconds). If dough is too moist to form a ball, add a bit more flour and process another few seconds, until dough is smooth and elastic. Or, combine ingredients in a second

medium-size bowl and stir with wooden spoon until dough is smooth and elastic.

4. Turn dough into greased bowl, cover with kitchen towel, and set aside to rise in warm place for 20 minutes.

5. Meanwhile, prick sausages in several places with fork and place in small skillet. Add enough cold water to cover and bring to a boil over high heat. Reduce heat and simmer sausages, uncovered, 15 minutes.

6. Drain sausages and set aside to cool.

7. Using food processor fitted with shredding disk, or coarse side of grater, shred mozzarella; set aside.

8. Cut sausages crosswise into ¼-inch-thick slices; set aside.

9. Arrange 2 racks approximately 3 inches apart in middle of oven and preheat oven to 450 degrees.

10. Rub four 8- or 9-inch metal pie pans, two 11 x 17-inch heavy-gauge cookie sheets, or a combination of both, with vegetable oil; set aside.

11. Turn dough out onto work surface and knead briefly. Divide into 4 equal portions and shape each into a smooth ball.

12. Lightly sprinkle work surface with cornmeal to prevent dough from sticking. Press and roll out each ball of dough into 8-inch round and place each round in prepared pie pan, or place 2 rounds on each cookie sheet.

13. Brush a 1-inch border of remaining olive oil around edge of each pizza. Pour ¼ cup of tomato sauce onto each pizza and spread evenly with back of spoon, leaving a ½-inch border free of sauce. Sprinkle each pizza with mozzarella and ¼ teaspoon oregano. Divide sausage among pizzas and bake 12 to 15 minutes, switching pans on shelves after 5 minutes to prevent the lower pizzas from burning.

14. To serve, cut each pizza into 6 wedges with a pizza wheel or chef's knife, or serve whole.

Sliced Oranges and Kiwis

3 navel oranges
3 kiwi fruits
¼ cup sour cream
1 tablespoon dark brown sugar

1. With sharp paring knife, cut ¼-inch-thick slice from stem end and base of each orange. Place orange firmly on plate and, using a downward sawing motion, cut away peel and as much white pith as possible, turning the fruit as you trim off each strip. Repeat for remaining oranges; discard peel.

2. Cut each orange crosswise into ¼-inch-thick rounds; set aside.

3. Using paring knife, remove peel from kiwis and discard. Cut kiwis crosswise into ¼-inch-thick rounds; set aside.

4. Divide orange and kiwi slices among 4 dessert plates, arranging them in a decorative pattern. Cover with plastic wrap and refrigerate until ready to serve.

5. Just before serving, top each dessert with a dollop of sour cream and sprinkle with brown sugar.

Italian-style Stuffed Peppers
Marinated Tomato and Red Onion Salad
Garlic Bread

Stuffed bell peppers, marinated tomato and red onion salad, and crusty garlic bread are an easy Italian meal.

Thick-skinned peppers are best for stuffing; choose those with relatively even bottoms so they do not topple over during baking. Look for peppers that are firm and shiny, with no signs of decay. They should feel hefty for their size. Be sure to remove all of the seeds before cooking because they are often bitter.

SHOPPING LIST AND STAPLES

4 to 5 sweet Italian sausages (about 1 pound total weight)
4 medium-size green bell peppers (about 1½ pounds total weight)
1 pound Italian plum tomatoes or other flavorful ripe tomatoes
Small yellow onion
Small red onion
2 cloves garlic
Small bunch fresh parsley
Small bunch fresh basil, or ¼ teaspoon dried
2 ounces Parmesan cheese
¾ cup plus 2 tablespoons olive oil, preferably fruity extra-virgin
1 tablespoon red wine vinegar
1 loaf Italian bread
2 slices firm home-style white bread
2-ounce jar pine nuts
Pinch of sugar
½ teaspoon dried oregano
Pinch of dry mustard
Salt
Freshly ground black pepper

UTENSILS

Food processor (optional)
Small skillet
Medium-size saucepan
Baking sheet
9 x 9-inch shallow baking dish
Shallow glass or ceramic dish
Large bowl
2 small bowls, 1 nonaluminum
Colander
Measuring cups and spoons
Chef's knife
Bread knife with serrated blade
Paring knife
Wooden spoon
Slotted spoon
Metal spatula
Small whisk
Pastry brush
Grater (if not using processor)

START-TO-FINISH STEPS

1. Peel and mince enough yellow onion to measure ⅓ cup for peppers recipe. For salad recipe, peel and cut 4 thin slices crosswise from red onion and separate into rings; mince enough remaining red onion to measure 2 tablespoons. Wash parsley, and fresh basil if using, and pat dry with paper towels. Trim stems from parsley and discard. Finely chop enough parsley to measure ⅓ cup for peppers recipe. Strip 12 basil leaves from stems. Coarsely chop 8 leaves for salad recipe and set aside 4 leaves for garnish. Reserve remaining herbs for another use.
2. Follow peppers recipe steps 1 through 8.
3. While peppers are baking, follow salad recipe steps 1 through 5.
4. Follow peppers recipe step 9.
5. While peppers finish baking, follow garlic bread recipe steps 1 through 4.
6. Follow peppers recipe step 10, turn on broiler, and follow garlic bread recipe step 5.
7. Follow salad recipe step 6, peppers recipe step 11, garlic bread recipe step 6, and serve.

RECIPES

Italian-style Stuffed Peppers

4 to 5 sweet Italian sausages (about 1 pound total weight)
2 ounces Parmesan cheese
2 slices firm home-style white bread
⅓ cup minced yellow onion
⅓ cup finely chopped fresh parsley
3 tablespoons pine nuts
½ teaspoon dried oregano
Pinch of freshly ground black pepper
4 medium-size green bell peppers (about 1½ pounds total weight)
2 tablespoons olive oil, preferably fruity extra-virgin

1. Preheat oven to 350 degrees.
2. Remove and discard sausage casings. Crumble sausage meat and place in large bowl.
3. In food processor fitted with steel blade, or with grater, grate enough Parmesan to measure ½ cup. Add ¼ cup Parmesan to bowl with sausage; set remainder aside.
4. Trim crusts from bread and discard. Using food processor, or coarse side of grater, grate enough bread to measure ½ cup plus 2 tablespoons crumbs. Add ½ cup crumbs to bowl with sausage and cheese; set remainder aside.
5. Add onion, parsley, pine nuts, oregano, and black pepper to sausage mixture and stir to combine.
6. Wash peppers and dry with paper towels. Cut ½-inch-thick slice from top of each pepper; remove and discard seeds. Mince edible parts of tops and add them to stuffing mixture.
7. Place peppers in 9 x 9-inch shallow baking dish. Divide stuffing among peppers, mounding it slightly if necessary, and drizzle with oil. Bake peppers 35 minutes.
8. Meanwhile, in small bowl, combine remaining ¼ cup Parmesan and 2 tablespoons bread crumbs; set aside.
9. Increase oven temperature to 375 degrees, sprinkle

peppers with Parmesan mixture, and bake another 10 minutes.

10. Remove peppers from oven, cover loosely with foil, and keep warm on stove top until ready to serve.

11. When ready to serve, using metal spatula, divide peppers among dinner plates.

Marinated Tomato and Red Onion Salad

1 pound Italian plum tomatoes or other flavorful ripe tomatoes
4 tablespoons olive oil, preferably fruity extra-virgin
1 tablespoon red wine vinegar
½ teaspoon salt
Pinch of sugar
Pinch of dry mustard
2 tablespoons minced red onion plus 4 thin slices, separated into rings
8 fresh basil leaves, coarsely chopped, plus 4 leaves for garnish, or ¼ teaspoon dried basil
¼ teaspoon freshly ground black pepper

1. Bring 1 quart of water to a boil in medium-size saucepan over high heat.

2. With paring knife, make small incision in base of each tomato. Plunge tomatoes into boiling water for 15 seconds. With slotted spoon, transfer tomatoes to colander and refresh under cold running water.

3. Meanwhile, in small nonaluminum bowl, combine oil, vinegar, salt, sugar, and dry mustard, and whisk until blended; set aside.

4. When tomatoes are cool enough to handle, remove skins and discard. Cut tomatoes crosswise into ½-inch-thick slices and arrange half of them in a single layer in shallow glass or ceramic dish. Sprinkle with half of the minced red onion, basil, and pepper. Top with remaining tomato slices and sprinkle with remaining minced onion, basil, and pepper. Top tomatoes with onion rings.

5. Whisk dressing to recombine and pour over salad. Set aside to marinate at least 15 minutes at room temperature.

6. Using slotted spoon, divide salad among 4 dinner plates and garnish each serving with a basil leaf.

Garlic Bread

1 loaf Italian bread
2 cloves garlic
½ cup olive oil, preferably fruity extra-virgin

Salt
Freshly ground black pepper

1. Halve bread lengthwise; set aside.

2. Crush garlic under flat blade of chef's knife. Remove peels and discard.

3. Rub cut surfaces of bread with crushed garlic; reserve garlic.

4. In small skillet, combine olive oil and garlic, and warm over low heat about 5 minutes.

5. Remove garlic from oil and discard. Brush cut surfaces of bread liberally with warm oil, sprinkle with salt and pepper to taste, and arrange bread, cut-side-up, on baking sheet. Place bread in preheated broiler 4 inches from heating element and toast 2 to 3 minutes, or until golden brown and crisp.

6. Remove bread from broiler. Cut on diagonal into 2-inch-wide pieces and divide among dinner plates or serve in napkin-lined basket.

ADDED TOUCH

This refreshing iced dessert—perfect for a hot summer evening—retains the flavor of fresh watermelon. If watermelon is out of season, substitute 1 quart of apple juice, and proceed with the recipe.

Watermelon Ice

5 pounds ripe watermelon
1 tablespoon freshly squeezed lemon juice
½ cup sugar, approximately

1. Using chef's knife, cut pulp from watermelon rind and place in large bowl; discard rind. Mash pulp with potato masher until completely broken down. In batches, force mashed pulp through sieve set over medium-size bowl, pressing with back of spoon. Or, beat pulp with electric mixer and then sieve. You should have about 1 quart juice.

2. Add lemon juice and sugar to taste to watermelon juice, and stir until sugar is dissolved.

3. Pour fruit syrup into ice-cream machine and freeze according to manufacturer's instructions. Or, pour into 2 metal ice-cube trays and freeze about 1 hour, or until mushy. Pour into food processor or blender and turn machine on and off 2 or 3 times to break up ice crystals. Return to ice-cube trays and refreeze. Repeat, if necessary, to achieve desired texture.

4. Divide ice among 4 bowls or goblets and serve.

Baked Ziti
Spinach Salad with Mushrooms and Homemade Croutons

Let everyone help themselves to baked ziti casserole and crisp spinach salad with mushrooms and croutons.

The ziti casserole combines some favorite children's foods—meatballs, pasta, and mild cheeses. This recipe will please busy parents, too. You can prepare the dish early in the day and cover and refrigerate it until baking time.

The accompanying iron-rich spinach salad with buttery croutons will also appeal to youngsters. If possible, buy loose spinach rather than the packaged type, which often contains many damaged leaves. Spinach should have a fresh odor; if there is any trace of a sour smell, do not buy it. The leaves should be fresh and dark green without wilt or bruises. Unwashed spinach can be refrigerated for up to 5 days, but it is best used as soon as possible. Before serving, rinse the spinach thoroughly. To stem the leaves, fold each in half lengthwise with the underside facing out, then pull off the stem.

SHOPPING LIST AND STAPLES

¾ pound lean ground chuck
1 pound fresh spinach
¾ pound mushrooms
Small bunch scallions
Small yellow onion
1 clove garlic
Small bunch parsley
1 lemon
28-ounce can Italian plum tomatoes in purée
6-ounce can tomato paste
1 egg
4 tablespoons unsalted butter
8-ounce package mozzarella cheese
8-ounce container whole-milk ricotta cheese
2 ounces Parmesan cheese
2 tablespoons olive oil
¾ pound ziti
1 loaf Italian bread, preferably stale
½ cup dry bread crumbs
Pinch of sugar
1 bay leaf
½ teaspoon dried oregano
½ teaspoon dried basil
Salt
Freshly ground black pepper

UTENSILS

Food processor (optional)
Stockpot or large saucepan
Medium-size skillet or sauté pan
Medium-size heavy-gauge nonaluminum saucepan or
    casserole
13 x 9 x 2-inch baking pan
Large salad bowl
Large bowl
Colander
Salad spinner (optional)
Measuring cups and spoons

Chef's knife
Paring knife
2 wooden spoons
Slotted spoon
Potato masher (optional)
Grater (if not using processor)

START-TO-FINISH STEPS

1. Follow ziti recipe steps 1 through 7.
2. While meatballs simmer, follow salad recipe steps 1 and 2.
3. Follow ziti recipe steps 8 through 13.
4. While ziti is baking, follow salad recipe steps 3 through 11.
5. Follow ziti recipe step 14 and serve with salad.

RECIPES

Baked Ziti

Small yellow onion
Small bunch parsley
2 tablespoons olive oil
2 ounces Parmesan cheese
28-ounce can Italian plum tomatoes in purée
¼ cup tomato paste
1 bay leaf
½ teaspoon dried oregano
½ teaspoon dried basil
Pinch of sugar
2 teaspoons salt
¼ teaspoon freshly ground black pepper
¾ pound lean ground chuck
½ cup dry bread crumbs
1 egg
8-ounce package mozzarella cheese
¾ pound ziti
1 cup whole-milk ricotta cheese

1. Halve and peel onion. Chop enough to measure ½ cup; set aside.
2. Wash parsley and dry with paper towels. Trim stems and discard. Chop enough parsley to measure ¾ cup; set aside.
3. Heat olive oil in medium-size heavy-gauge non-aluminum saucepan or casserole over medium heat. Add chopped onion and sauté, stirring occasionally, 2 minutes, or until softened but not browned.
4. Meanwhile, grate enough Parmesan in food processor or with grater to measure ¼ cup; set aside.
5. Add tomatoes with purée to pan and stir, crushing tomatoes with edge of spoon or potato masher. Stir in tomato paste, bay leaf, oregano, basil, sugar, ½ teaspoon salt, and ⅛ teaspoon pepper, and bring to a gentle boil.
6. Crumble ground meat into large bowl. Add ½ cup of the parsley, bread crumbs, grated Parmesan, ½ teaspoon salt, and remaining ⅛ teaspoon pepper. Add egg and stir with fork until mixture is well combined. With wet hands,

shape mixture into 1-inch meatballs. You will have about 30 meatballs.

7. Stir sauce to be sure it is not sticking to bottom of pan. Drop meatballs into boiling sauce and simmer gently, uncovered, turning meatballs occasionally but not stirring, 20 minutes.

8. Preheat oven to 375 degrees.

9. Bring 3 quarts of water and 1 teaspoon salt to a boil in stockpot or large saucepan.

10. While water is heating, shred mozzarella in food processor fitted with shredding disk, or with grater; set aside.

11. Stir ziti into boiling water and cook about 9 minutes, or just until *al dente*. Do *not* overcook.

12. Turn ziti into colander and drain well.

13. Remove bay leaf from sauce and discard. Spoon off any fat from the surface before proceeding. Turn half of the tomato sauce and meatballs into 13 x 9 x 2-inch baking pan. Spread ziti over sauce. Top ziti with mozzarella and remaining sauce and meatballs. Dot with spoonsful of ricotta cheese and bake 20 minutes, or until piping hot.

14. Sprinkle baked ziti with remaining ¼ cup parsley and serve from baking pan.

Spinach Salad with Mushrooms and Homemade Croutons

1 pound fresh spinach
Small bunch scallions
1 clove garlic
1 loaf Italian bread, preferably stale
4 tablespoons unsalted butter
¾ pound mushrooms
1 lemon
¼ teaspoon salt
Pinch of freshly ground black pepper

1. Wash spinach thoroughly in several changes of cold water. Dry in salad spinner or with paper towels. Remove and discard any bruised or discolored leaves. Remove tough stems and discard. Tear enough spinach leaves into bite-size pieces to measure 4 cups and place in large salad bowl.

2. Wash scallions and dry with paper towels. Trim ends and discard. Cut enough scallions crosswise into ¼-inch pieces to measure ½ cup. Add sliced scallions to bowl with spinach, cover with plastic wrap, and refrigerate until ready to serve. Reserve remaining scallions for another use.

3. Crush garlic under flat blade of chef's knife. Remove peel and discard. Set garlic aside.

4. Cut enough bread into ½-inch cubes to measure 1 cup; reserve remainder for another use.

5. Combine garlic and 2 tablespoons butter in medium-size skillet or sauté pan over medium heat. When foaming subsides, remove and discard garlic. Add bread cubes and sauté, stirring occasionally, about 5 minutes, or until crisp and golden.

6. Meanwhile, wipe mushrooms clean with damp paper towels. Cut mushrooms into ⅛-inch-thick slices; set aside. You should have about 3 cups sliced mushrooms.

7. With slotted spoon, transfer croutons to paper-towel-lined plate; set aside.

8. Add remaining butter to skillet and melt over medium heat. When foaming subsides, add mushrooms and sauté, stirring occasionally, about 7 minutes, or until the liquid they yield has evaporated and mushrooms are beginning to brown at the edges.

9. Remove pan from heat and set aside.

10. Squeeze enough lemon juice to measure 2 tablespoons.

11. Add lemon juice, salt, and pepper to spinach and scallions, and toss to combine. Add croutons and mushrooms, and toss.

ADDED TOUCH

Tortoni is an Italian ice cream with a mousse-like consistency. Here, the cook adds gingersnap crumbs to the mixture for extra flavor.

Gingersnap Tortoni

Seven 2-inch gingersnaps
1 egg
¼ cup confectioners' sugar
1 cup heavy cream, well chilled
½ teaspoon vanilla extract
2 tablespoons blanched slivered almonds

1. Place gingersnaps between 2 sheets of waxed paper and crush with rolling pin. Measure out ½ cup crumbs and set aside.

2. Separate egg, placing white in medium-size bowl and reserving yolk for another use. With electric mixer set at high speed, beat egg white until soft peaks form. Add 1 tablespoon sugar and beat until stiff but not dry; set aside.

3. Combine cream, vanilla, and remaining 3 tablespoons sugar in another medium-size bowl and beat with mixer at high speed until stiff peaks form.

4. With rubber spatula, gently fold beaten egg white into whipped cream. Sprinkle mixture with ½ of the gingersnap crumbs and fold in gently. Do *not* beat or overfold.

5. Divide mixture among four 8-ounce ramekins and tap each on counter to settle mixture. Cover each serving with waxed paper and freeze 1½ to 2 hours, or until solid, or leave in freezer overnight.

6. Preheat oven to 350 degrees.

7. Arrange almonds in single layer on baking sheet and toast in oven, shaking pan occasionally to prevent scorching, 5 to 8 minutes, or until light golden.

8. Remove almonds from oven and set aside to cool slightly.

9. Just before serving, remove desserts from freezer and sprinkle each with toasted almonds. If desired, place in refrigerator for 10 minutes to soften.

Ann Burckhardt

L ike most working mothers, Ann Burckhardt finds time a precious commodity. An early cooking mentor taught her to question the role each ingredient plays in a recipe: If an ingredient is not absolutely necessary, omit it and save the cost and the time needed to obtain, measure, and add it. For instance, the dough that wraps the hot dogs in Menu 2 consists of just two ingredients—self-rising flour and cream—rather than the butter, flour, baking powder, salt, and water that a standard pastry might require.

All of Ann Burckhardt's menus reflect this efficient approach to cooking. Menu 1 is a simple meal that can be served at any time of year. The main-course soup—made with carrot, onion, zucchini, and ham—is rich, yet light enough to be enjoyed in warm weather or cold. Here it is paired with airy popovers and a creamy Cheddar cheese spread.

In Menu 2, she offers hot dogs baked in pastry—more popularly known as pigs in blankets. When served with ketchup or chili sauce and mustard for dipping, they make ideal fare for a weekday supper or a child's birthday party. Corn on the cob cut into wheels and coleslaw with yogurt-mayonnaise dressing are the perfect partners for the hot dogs.

Menu 3 has Swedish origins. Baked acorn squash halves are filled with tiny meatballs in a rich sauce and accompanied by scones flavored with orange rind, anise, and fennel. The scones are an adaptation of the popular Scandinavian rye bread called *limpa*.

This family meal features an appetizing vegetable-ham soup and popovers with a mustardy Cheddar cheese spread. The popovers should be served hot, so seat everyone first, and then bring out the dinner.

Vegetable Soup with Ham
Popovers
Creamy Cheddar Spread

Popovers, unlike other quick breads, require no leavening agent to make them rise. They achieve their puffiness from the high proportion of liquid in the batter, which is converted to steam as the popovers bake in the hot oven. To get the most expansion, beat the batter until it has the consistency of heavy cream, and use a popover pan or aluminum muffin pan that has cups that are deeper than they are wide so the batter can expand only upward. Because popovers double in size when baked, very little batter is needed in each cup (divide the batter evenly among the cups, whether you use an 8-cup or a 12-cup pan). Preheating the pan sets the bottoms of the popovers and speeds the rising. Because popovers are fragile and can collapse if exposed to a sudden draft, do not open the oven door to peek at them until they are finished baking.

SHOPPING LIST AND STAPLES

¼ pound cooked ham, sliced
Medium-size zucchini (about ½ pound)
2 large carrots (about ½ pound total weight)
Medium-size yellow onion plus small yellow onion
Small bunch parsley
2½ cups chicken stock, preferably homemade (see page 12), or canned
3 large eggs
1½ cups milk, approximately
1 pint half-and-half
1 stick unsalted butter
¼ pound sharp Cheddar cheese
8-ounce package cream cheese
¼ cup vegetable oil
1 teaspoon Dijon mustard
1 cup plus 6 tablespoons all-purpose or unbleached flour
¼ cup yellow cornmeal
1½ teaspoons sweet Hungarian paprika, approximately
Salt

UTENSILS

Food processor or blender (optional)
Stockpot or large heavy-gauge saucepan with cover
Medium-size saucepan with cover
8-cup heavy-gauge popover pan or 12-cup muffin pan
2 medium-size bowls
Small bowl
Strainer
Measuring cups and spoons
Chef's knife
Paring knife
Wooden spoon
Slotted spoon
Rubber spatula
Wire whisk
Vegetable peeler
Ladle
Pastry brush
Vegetable brush
Grater (if not using processor)
Sifter

START-TO-FINISH STEPS

One hour ahead: Set out eggs for popovers recipe and butter and cheeses for Cheddar spread recipe to come to room temperature.

1. Follow Cheddar spread recipe steps 1 through 5.
2. Follow soup recipe steps 1 through 5.
3. Follow popovers recipe steps 1 through 7.
4. While popovers are baking, follow soup recipe steps 6 through 15.
5. Follow popovers recipe step 8, soup recipe step 16, and serve with Cheddar spread.

RECIPES

Vegetable Soup with Ham

2 large carrots (about ½ pound total weight)
Medium-size zucchini (about ½ pound)
Medium-size yellow onion,
Small bunch parsley
2½ cups chicken stock
¼ pound cooked ham, sliced
6 tablespoons unsalted butter
6 tablespoons all-purpose or unbleached flour
1½ cups half-and-half

1. Peel and trim carrots. Halve carrots lengthwise, then cut crosswise into 1-inch pieces.
2. Scrub zucchini under cold running water and dry with paper towels. Trim ends and discard. Halve lengthwise,

30

then cut crosswise into 1-inch pieces.

3. Peel and quarter onion.

4. Using food processor or chef's knife, coarsely chop vegetables.

5. Wash parsley and dry with paper towels. Trim stems and discard. Mince enough parsley to measure ¼ cup and set aside; reserve remainder for another use.

6. Combine chopped vegetables and stock in medium-size saucepan and bring to a boil over medium-high heat. Reduce heat to medium, cover pan, and simmer about 10 minutes, or until vegetables are tender.

7. Meanwhile, stack ham slices and cut into thin strips.

8. Melt butter in stockpot over medium-high heat. Add ham strips and sauté, stirring frequently, 2 to 3 minutes.

9. With slotted spoon, transfer ham to small bowl and set aside.

10. Reduce heat under stockpot to low, add flour to butter remaining in pot, and whisk until blended. Cook mixture, stirring constantly, 30 seconds, or until it is smooth and bubbly.

11. Remove stockpot from heat. Whisking continuously, gradually add half-and-half and whisk until well blended and smooth.

12. Return stockpot to medium-high heat and bring soup base to a boil, stirring constantly. Boil 1 minute and remove pan from heat.

13. When vegetables are tender, pour stock through strainer set over medium-size bowl; set stock aside.

14. Turn cooked vegetables into container of food processor fitted with steel blade and pulse machine on and off once or twice to mince vegetables. Or, mince vegetables with chef's knife.

15. Stir minced vegetables, ham, and 2 cups of reserved stock into soup base and bring to a simmer over low heat.

16. Divide soup among 4 bowls, sprinkle each serving with parsley, and serve.

Popovers

1¼ cups milk
3 tablespoons vegetable oil, approximately
½ teaspoon salt
1 cup all-purpose or unbleached flour
¼ cup yellow cornmeal
3 large eggs, at room temperature

1. Preheat oven to 425 degrees.

2. Heat 8-cup heavy-gauge popover pan or 12-cup muffin pan in oven while preparing batter.

3. For batter, combine milk, 2 tablespoons oil, and salt in medium-size bowl.

4. Combine flour and cornmeal in sifter and sift into bowl with liquid ingredients. With wire whisk, beat mixture about 1 minute, or until smooth.

5. Add eggs, one at a time, beating after each addition just until incorporated; do *not* overbeat. Set batter aside.

6. Remove pan from oven and, using pastry brush, coat cups with remaining oil.

7. Divide batter among cups of popover or muffin pan and bake 20 to 25 minutes, or until popovers are puffed, golden, and crisp. Do not open oven door until popovers are ready.

8. Remove popovers from pan and serve. Do not cover them or they will become soggy.

Creamy Cheddar Spread

¼ pound sharp Cheddar cheese, at room temperature
Small yellow onion
8-ounce package cream cheese, at room temperature
2 tablespoons milk
2 tablespoons unsalted butter, at room temperature
1 teaspoon Dijon mustard
1½ teaspoons sweet Hungarian paprika, approximately

1. In food processor fitted with shredding disk, or with grater, shred Cheddar cheese. Transfer cheese to sheet of waxed paper.

2. Halve and peel onion. In food processor fitted with steel blade, or with chef's knife, mince enough onion to measure 1 tablespoon; reserve remaining onion for another use.

3. In food processor fitted with steel blade or in blender, combine shredded Cheddar, cream cheese, onion, milk, butter, and mustard, and process until smooth.

4. With machine running, add paprika, ¼ teaspoon at a time, adding just enough to give mixture a rosy hue.

5. Divide cheese spread among 4 small ramekins or turn into small serving bowl, cover with plastic wrap, and refrigerate until ready to serve.

LEFTOVER SUGGESTION

Scoop any remaining cheese spread into an airtight container and refrigerate it for up to a week. The spread makes a zesty alternative to mayonnaise for sandwiches.

Pigs in Blankets
Corn Wheels
Coleslaw with Yogurt Mayonnaise

Youngsters and adults alike will love this all-American meal of pigs in blankets, corn wheels, and creamy coleslaw.

Corn on the cob is a food beloved by Americans of all ages. If possible, buy corn at a farm stand the same day it is picked, and cook it as soon as you can before its sugar turns to starch. No matter where you buy fresh corn, look for bright green husks and unwilted silk. The kernels should be of uniform color and in regular rows, and the ears should have no odor. Cooking the corn in milk and butter keeps it sweet and tender.

SHOPPING LIST AND STAPLES

1-pound package hot dogs
4 to 6 ears fresh corn on the cob
Small head green cabbage (about 1 pound)
Large carrot
Small bunch scallions
3 cups low-fat milk
½ pint heavy cream
8-ounce container plain yogurt
1 stick unsalted butter
¼ cup mayonnaise

14-ounce bottle ketchup or 12-ounce bottle chili sauce
   (optional)
8-ounce jar mustard (optional)
1 cup self-rising flour
8-ounce jar salted peanuts
Salt

UTENSILS

Food processor or grater
Large nonaluminum saucepan with cover
Small heavy-gauge saucepan or butter warmer
Baking pan
Salad bowl
Medium-size bowl
2 small bowls
Measuring cups and spoons
Chef's knife
Paring knife
2 wooden spoons
Rubber spatula

Metal tongs
Pastry brush
Rolling pin

START-TO-FINISH STEPS

1. Follow coleslaw recipe steps 1 through 5.
2. Follow pigs in blankets recipe step 1 and corn recipe step 1.
3. Follow pigs in blankets recipe steps 2 through 6.
4. While pigs in blankets are baking, follow corn recipe step 2 and coleslaw recipe step 6.
5. Follow corn recipe steps 3 and 4.
6. While butter is melting, follow pigs in blankets recipe step 7.
7. Follow coleslaw recipe step 7, pigs in blankets recipe step 8, corn recipe step 5, and serve.

RECIPES

Pigs in Blankets

1 cup self-rising flour
⅔ to ¾ cup heavy cream
8 hot dogs
14-ounce bottle ketchup or 12-ounce bottle chili sauce
   (optional)
8-ounce jar mustard (optional)

1. Preheat oven to 425 degrees.
2. In medium-size bowl, combine flour with enough cream to form a soft dough.
3. Turn dough out onto lightly floured surface and knead twelve times.
4. Roll dough out into 7 by 10-inch rectangle. Cut in half horizontally, then cut vertically into quarters, forming 8 "blankets."
5. Place a hot dog along one short edge of a blanket, roll up, and seal tightly by pinching dough together. Place seam-side-down on ungreased baking pan. Repeat for remaining hot dogs.
6. Bake pigs in blankets 12 to 15 minutes, or until dough is golden brown.
7. Turn ketchup or chili sauce and mustard, if using, into individual serving bowls; set aside.
8. Transfer pigs in blankets to platter and serve with ketchup or chili sauce and mustard, if desired.

Corn Wheels

4 to 6 ears fresh corn on the cob
3 cups low-fat milk
1 stick unsalted butter

1. Shuck corn; remove and discard silk. Cut each ear crosswise into 1½-inch-wide "wheels."
2. Combine milk, 4 tablespoons butter, and 1 quart water in large nonaluminum saucepan and bring to a boil over high heat.
3. Add corn and boil, partially covered, 5 to 8 minutes, or until fork tender.
4. Meanwhile, melt remaining 4 tablespoons butter in small heavy-gauge saucepan or butter warmer over low heat.
5. Using metal tongs, transfer corn to serving bowl and brush generously with melted butter.

Coleslaw with Yogurt Mayonnaise

Small head green cabbage (about 1 pound)
Large carrot
Small bunch scallions
¼ cup plain yogurt
¼ cup mayonnaise
¼ teaspoon salt
¼ cup salted peanuts

1. Remove and discard bruised and discolored outer leaves from cabbage. Quarter cabbage lengthwise; remove and discard core. Using food processor fitted with shredding disk, or coarse side of grater, shred enough cabbage to measure 2 cups; transfer to salad bowl. Reserve remaining cabbage for another use.
2. Peel and trim carrot. Using food processor fitted with steel blade, or coarse side of grater, shred enough carrot to measure 1 cup; add to bowl with cabbage.
3. Wash scallions and dry with paper towels. Trim ends and discard. Chop enough scallions to measure 2 tablespoons; add to bowl with cabbage and shredded carrot. Reserve remaining scallions for another use.
4. For dressing, combine yogurt, mayonnaise, and salt in small bowl and stir until well blended.
5. Add dressing to vegetables and toss until evenly coated. Cover with plastic wrap and refrigerate until ready to serve.
6. Coarsely chop peanuts; set aside.
7. Just before serving, sprinkle coleslaw with peanuts.

Swedish Meatballs in Acorn Squash
Limpa Scones

Apple-patterned dinnerware sets an autumnal mood for acorn squash halves heaped with meatballs and gravy. Serve the honey-sweetened rye scones right from the oven in a napkin-lined basket.

Baking acorn squash preserves its full flavor. Select squash that is firm, heavy, and free of cracks or decay. You can fill the squash halves with the Swedish meatballs and sauce, or serve the filling separately.

SHOPPING LIST AND STAPLES

1 pound ground beef round
2 small acorn squash (about 2 pounds total weight)
Small white or yellow onion
1 orange
1 cup beef stock, preferably homemade (see page 12), or canned
2 eggs
½ cup milk
¾ cup buttermilk
½ pint heavy cream
2 tablespoons plus 2 teaspoons unsalted butter
¼ cup plus 1 tablespoon vegetable oil
2 tablespoons honey or molasses
1 slice firm home-style white bread
1 cup self-rising flour
3 tablespoons all-purpose flour
1 cup medium rye flour
¼ teaspoon baking soda
1 teaspoon fennel seeds
½ teaspoon anise seeds
½ teaspoon freshly grated nutmeg
Salt
Freshly ground pepper

UTENSILS

Food processor (optional)
14-inch heavy-gauge skillet or 2 medium-size skillets
1½-quart ovenproof casserole with cover
11 x 7 x 1½-inch baking pan
17 x 11-inch baking sheet
Large bowl (if not using processor)
Medium-size bowl
2 small bowls, 1 heatproof
Measuring cups and spoons
Chef's knife
Paring knife
Wooden spoon
Slotted spoon
Small spatula

Wire whisk
Grater
Sifter
Mortar and pestle (optional)
Rolling pin (if not using mortar and pestle)

START-TO-FINISH STEPS

1. Follow meatballs recipe steps 1 through 13 and increase oven temperature to 425 degrees.
2. Follow scones recipe steps 1 through 8.
3. Follow meatballs recipe step 14, scones recipe step 9, and serve.

RECIPES

Swedish Meatballs in Acorn Squash

2 small acorn squash (about 2 pounds total
  weight)
Small white or yellow onion
1 slice firm home-style bread
1 pound ground beef round
1 egg
½ cup milk
½ teaspoon freshly grated nutmeg
1 teaspoon salt
Freshly ground pepper
2 tablespoons plus 2 teaspoons unsalted butter
3 tablespoons all-purpose flour
1 cup beef stock
½ cup heavy cream

1. Preheat oven to 400 degrees.
2. Halve squash lengthwise; scoop out seeds and strings, and discard. Place squash halves cut-side-down in 11 by 7 by 1½-inch baking pan. Fill pan to a depth of ¼ inch with hot tap water and bake squash, uncovered, 30 minutes, or until fork tender.
3. Meanwhile, peel and quarter onion. In food processor fitted with steel blade, chop enough onion to measure ½ cup. Or, mince onion with chef's knife and place in large bowl.
4. Trim crusts from bread and discard. Tear bread into small pieces and add to onions.
5. Crumble meat and add to onions and bread.
6. Add egg, milk, and nutmeg to meat mixture in processor, season with salt and pepper, and pulse machine on and off a few times, just until mixture is combined. Or, blend mixture with your hands; do *not* overwork mixture.
7. Heat 2 tablespoons butter in large heavy-gauge skillet or 1 tablespoon butter in each of 2 medium-size skillets over medium-high heat.
8. While butter is heating, begin shaping meatballs: Using two teaspoons, scoop up a heaping teaspoonful of meat mixture in one spoon, then roll meat off spoon into skillet with second teaspoon. Working quickly, repeat process with remaining meat mixture. You will have approximately 28 meatballs. Brown meatballs, turning occasion-

ally with small spatula, about 15 minutes, or until evenly browned.
9. With slotted spoon, transfer meatballs to ovenproof casserole and pour fat from skillet into small heatproof bowl.
10. Return 2 tablespoons fat to skillet. Whisk in flour and cook mixture over medium heat, whisking constantly, 1 to 2 minutes, or until bubbly.
11. Add stock to skillet and continue cooking, stirring occasionally, about 3 minutes, or until sauce thickens.
12. Reduce heat to low, add cream, and whisk until blended. Pour sauce over meatballs, cover casserole, and keep warm on stove top until ready to serve.
13. When squash is done, remove from oven and turn cut-side-up. Using paring knife, crosshatch flesh of each half and dot each with ½ teaspoon butter. Cover loosely with aluminum foil and keep warm on stove top until ready to serve.
14. Divide squash halves among 4 dinner plates and fill cavity of each with meatballs and sauce.

Limpa Scones

¼ cup plus 1 tablespoon vegetable oil
1 orange
1 teaspoon fennel seeds
½ teaspoon anise seeds
1 cup self-rising flour
1 cup medium rye flour
¼ teaspoon baking soda
1 egg
2 tablespoons honey or molasses
¾ cup buttermilk

1. Lightly grease 17 by 11-inch baking sheet; set aside.
2. Wash orange and dry with paper towel. Grate enough orange rind to measure 1 tablespoon; set aside. Reserve orange for another use.
3. Crush fennel and anise seeds in mortar with pestle. Or, place seeds between 2 sheets of waxed paper and crush with rolling pin. Set seeds aside.
4. Sift self-rising and rye flours into medium-size bowl. Stir in baking soda; set aside.
5. In small bowl, beat egg with fork just until blended. Stir in ¼ cup vegetable oil, honey or molasses, buttermilk, crushed fennel seeds, anise seeds, and grated orange rind.
6. Add buttermilk mixture to dry ingredients and mix quickly with fork, until mixture holds together.
7. Using sharp knife, cut dough in half. Turn half the dough out onto one corner of prepared baking sheet; turn other half out onto opposite corner of sheet. With floured fingers, pat dough out into two 8-inch rounds, about ½-inch thick. With knife dipped in flour, cut each round into 6 wedges, but do not separate.
8. Bake scones in preheated 425-degree oven 10 to 15 minutes, or until lightly browned.
9. Remove scones from oven, separate wedges, and turn into napkin-lined basket.

Lucy Wing

Although Lucy Wing grew up eating traditional Chinese food, she describes herself as an eclectic cook with an international palate. She particularly enjoys simplifying recipes from many lands and cooking quickly to preserve the natural flavors of foods. Her family menus feature basic dishes with some new twists.

In Menu 1, macaroni and cheese, an all-American favorite, takes on southwestern flair with the addition of diced mild green chilies and a topping of tomato sauce, grated cheese, scallions, and olives. An avocado and vegetable salad and Mexican-style hot chocolate are served with the casserole.

Menus 2 and 3 will please children and adults alike. Menu 2 offers broiled steak marinated in a tangy vinegar and herb mixture. The cook accompanies the meat with her own version of home fries in which the potato slices are sautéed and then baked for extra crispness.

Menu 3 is a quick and easy midweek meal that features whole-wheat pizza made with a quick-bread crust that does not require time to rise. The pizza is topped with a variety of traditional ingredients—mozzarella cheese, tomato sauce, mushrooms, green peppers, and pepperoni— and presented with a colorful three-bean salad.

Bright tableware sets off this colorful southwestern meal of macaroni and cheese casserole and California-style salad. Mugs of spiced Mexican hot chocolate add sweetness.

Tex-Mex Macaroni and Cheese
California Salad
Mexican Hot Chocolate

For the macaroni and cheese dish, the cook prefers Longhorn, a type of mild Cheddar named for its long, cylindrical shape. It has a yellow-gold color and is often coated with wax for protection. Produced in the Midwest, it is available at cheese stores throughout the country.

The fitting beverage for this Tex-Mex meal is Mexican-style hot chocolate, which is spiced with cinnamon and whisked before serving. For an extra-frothy drink, pour one cup of the hot chocolate into a blender and whip until foamy. Return the beaten chocolate to the pan, add the vanilla, and serve.

SHOPPING LIST AND STAPLES

1 head iceberg lettuce
Large ripe avocado, preferably Hass variety
Small cucumber
Small bunch red radishes
Small bunch scallions
Large lemon
8-ounce can tomato sauce
4-ounce can diced mild green chilies
3½-ounce can pitted black olives (optional)
1 quart plus 2 cups milk
½ pint heavy cream
2 tablespoons unsalted butter
½ pound Longhorn or other mild Cheddar cheese
½ cup olive or vegetable oil, approximately
1 teaspoon Worcestershire sauce
8 ounces elbow macaroni
¼ cup sugar, approximately
3 tablespoons all-purpose flour
2 ounces (2 squares) semisweet chocolate
1 teaspoon vanilla extract
1 teaspoon dry mustard
1 teaspoon chili powder
½ teaspoon cinnamon
½ teaspoon dried tarragon
Dash of Cayenne pepper
Salt

UTENSILS

Food processor (optional)
Large saucepan or stockpot
2 medium-size heavy-gauge nonaluminum saucepans

Small nonaluminum saucepan with cover
Shallow 1½-quart baking dish
Small bowl
Colander
Strainer
Salad spinner (optional)
Measuring cups and spoons
Chef's knife
Paring knife
2 wooden spoons
Rubber spatula
Whisk
Small jar with tight-fitting lid
Citrus juicer (optional)
Grater (if not using processor)
Electric mixer

START-TO-FINISH STEPS

1. Follow hot chocolate recipe step 1.
2. Follow salad recipe steps 1 through 7.
3. Follow hot chocolate recipe step 2.
4. Follow macaroni recipe steps 1 through 17.
5. Follow hot chocolate recipe steps 3 through 5.
6. Follow salad recipe step 8, macaroni recipe step 18, and serve with hot chocolate.

RECIPES

Tex-Mex Macaroni and Cheese

½ pound Longhorn or other mild Cheddar cheese
4-ounce can diced mild green chilies
2 cups elbow macaroni
2 tablespoons unsalted butter
3 tablespoons all-purpose flour
1 teaspoon dry mustard
½ teaspoon salt
2 cups milk
1 teaspoon Worcestershire sauce
Small bunch scallions
1 tablespoon olive or vegetable oil
1 teaspoon chili powder
8-ounce can tomato sauce
3½-ounce can pitted black olives (optional)

1. Preheat oven to 375 degrees.
2. Bring 3 quarts water to a boil in large saucepan or stockpot over high heat.
3. While water is heating, shred enough cheese in food processor fitted with shredding disk, or with grater, to measure 2 cups; set aside.
4. Turn chilies into strainer and rinse under cold running water. Drain and pat dry with paper towels. Set aside 3 to 4 tablespoons chilies and reserve remainder for another use.
5. Add elbow macaroni to boiling water, stir to separate, and cook 8 to 12 minutes, or according to package directions.
6. Meanwhile, melt butter in medium-size nonaluminum saucepan over medium heat. Whisk in flour, mustard, and salt.
7. Remove pan from heat. Whisking continuously, gradually add milk and whisk until well blended.
8. Return pan to heat and cook, stirring constantly, 2 to 3 minutes, or until sauce thickens.
9. Reduce heat to low and simmer sauce 1 minute.
10. Meanwhile, grease shallow 1½-quart baking dish; set aside.
11. Remove sauce from heat. Stir in 1½ cups shredded cheese, chilies, and Worcestershire sauce, and continue stirring 1 to 2 minutes, or until cheese is completely melted; set aside.
12. Turn macaroni into colander and drain. Return macaroni to large saucepan or stockpot, add cheese sauce, and toss to combine.
13. Turn macaroni and cheese into prepared baking dish, smooth top, and bake 25 to 30 minutes, or until sauce is bubbly.
14. Meanwhile, wash scallions and dry with paper towels. Trim ends and discard. Finely chop enough scallions to measure ¼ cup, and cut enough remaining scallions crosswise into ¼-inch pieces to measure ¼ cup for garnish, if using. Reserve any remaining scallions for another use.
15. Heat oil in small nonaluminum saucepan over medium heat. Add ¼ cup chopped scallions and chili powder, and sauté 1 minute.
16. Stir in tomato sauce and bring to a boil. Reduce heat to low and simmer, partially covered, 10 minutes.
17. Drain olives, if using, and slice enough to measure ¼ cup; set aside.
18. Remove baked macaroni from oven, spoon tomato sauce over center, and top with remaining ½ cup cheese. Sprinkle with scallion pieces and olive slices if desired, and serve.

California Salad

Large lemon
⅓ cup olive or vegetable oil
½ teaspoon dried tarragon
¼ teaspoon salt
Dash of Cayenne pepper

1 head iceberg lettuce
Large ripe avocado, preferably Hass variety
Small cucumber
Small bunch red radishes

1. Halve lemon crosswise and squeeze enough juice to measure 3 tablespoons.
2. To prepare dressing, combine 2 tablespoons lemon juice, oil, tarragon, salt, and Cayenne pepper in small jar with tight-fitting lid, and shake until well blended; set aside.
3. Remove any bruised or discolored outer leaves from lettuce. Halve lettuce lengthwise; cut out core from each half and discard. Rinse lettuce under cold running water and dry in salad spinner or with paper towels. Cut enough lettuce crosswise into ¼-inch-wide shreds to measure about 8 cups. Divide lettuce among 4 salad plates; set aside.
4. Halve avocado lengthwise. Twist halves to separate; remove and discard pit. Peel avocado. Cut each half lengthwise into 8 slices and arrange in single layer on large plate. Sprinkle avocado with remaining lemon juice to prevent discoloration and turn slices to coat evenly. Divide avocado slices among lettuce-lined plates.
5. Wash cucumber and dry with paper towel. With fork, score peel lengthwise. Cut enough cucumber crosswise into ¼-inch-thick slices to measure ¾ cup. Top each salad with equal portions of cucumber slices.
6. Wash and trim radishes; dry with paper towels. Cut enough radishes crosswise into ¼-inch-thick slices to measure ½ cup and divide among salads. Reserve remaining radishes for another use.
7. Cover salads with plastic wrap and refrigerate until ready to serve.
8. Just before serving, shake dressing to recombine and pour an equal amount over each salad.

Mexican Hot Chocolate

½ cup heavy cream
2 ounces (2 squares) semisweet chocolate
½ teaspoon cinnamon
2 tablespoons to ¼ cup sugar
1 quart milk
1 teaspoon vanilla extract

1. Place small bowl and beaters for whipping cream in freezer to chill, about 10 minutes.
2. Pour cream into chilled bowl and beat with electric mixer at high speed until stiff. Cover with plastic wrap and refrigerate until ready to serve.
3. Melt chocolate in medium-size heavy-gauge saucepan over low heat.
4. Whisk in cinnamon, and sugar to taste. Whisking continuously, add milk gradually and heat about 5 minutes, or until chocolate is hot and slightly foamy.
5. Stir in vanilla extract. Divide hot chocolate among 4 mugs and top each serving with a dollop of whipped cream.

Herb-Marinated Steak
Home Fries
Broiled Summer Squash and Tomatoes

S teak and potatoes are always a good family meal. Here the potatoes are left unpared to save time and to preserve the nutrients found just beneath the potato skins. After sautéing, the potatoes finish browning in the oven and need no further attention.

Zucchini and yellow squash are at their peak during the summer, but are often available in supermarkets in other seasons. You can use zucchini alone, if necessary. Select small, plump squash with glossy, unblemished skins. Avoid any that are very large; they tend to be bland and

Turn a family dinner into a special occasion with marinated broiled steak—cooked indoors or out—accompanied by golden-brown potato slices and bread-crumb-topped summer vegetables. Tumblers of iced tea refresh the palate.

seedy. If you must purchase the squash a few days in advance, store them in a perforated plastic bag in the refrigerator.

SHOPPING LIST AND STAPLES

1½-pound 1-inch-thick boneless sirloin steak
2 pounds Idaho potatoes
4 small tomatoes (about 1½ pounds
   total weight)
2 small zucchini (about ¾ pound
   total weight)
2 small yellow squash (about ¾ pound
   total weight)
Small clove garlic

1 stick plus 1 tablespoon unsalted butter
¼ cup olive oil
⅓ cup red wine vinegar
⅓ cup soy sauce
⅓ cup Worcestershire sauce
⅓ cup seasoned dry bread crumbs
¼ cup light brown sugar, firmly packed
1 teaspoon dried oregano
½ teaspoon dried basil
Salt
Freshly ground black pepper

UTENSILS

Large sauté pan
Broiler pan with rack
13 x 9 x 2-inch glass or ceramic dish
Small shallow baking dish
Small saucepan
2 serving platters
Measuring cups and spoons
Chef's knife
Carving knife
Paring knife
Wooden spoon
Slotted spatula
Vegetable brush
Metal tongs
Basting brush

START-TO-FINISH STEPS

1. Follow steak recipe step 1 and home fries recipe steps 1 through 5.
2. While potatoes are baking, follow vegetables recipe steps 1 through 4.
3. Follow home fries recipe step 6 and vegetables recipe steps 5 through 10.
4. Follow steak recipe steps 2 through 5 and serve with home fries and vegetables.

RECIPES

Herb-Marinated Steak

⅓ cup red wine vinegar
⅓ cup soy sauce
⅓ cup Worcestershire sauce
¼ cup light brown sugar, firmly packed
1 teaspoon dried oregano
½ teaspoon dried basil
1½-pound 1-inch-thick boneless sirloin steak

1. Combine vinegar, soy sauce, Worcestershire sauce, brown sugar, oregano, and basil in 13 x 9 x 2-inch glass or ceramic dish. Add steak and set aside to marinate about 30 minutes at room temperature.
2. Transfer steak to broiler rack set 4 inches from heating element in preheated broiler and broil on one side, 7 minutes for rare, 8 minutes for medium, or 10 minutes for well done. Reserve marinade.
3. Using metal tongs, turn steak, brush with marinade, and broil another 7 to 10 minutes for desired degree of doneness.
4. Transfer steak to serving platter, cover loosely with foil, and allow to rest 5 minutes.
5. Slice steak and serve.

Home Fries

2 pounds Idaho potatoes
4 tablespoons unsalted butter
¼ cup olive oil
Salt and freshly ground black pepper

1. Preheat oven to 475 degrees.
2. With vegetable brush, scrub potatoes under cold running water. Rinse and dry with paper towels; do *not* peel. Cut enough potatoes crosswise into ⅛-inch-thick slices to measure about 6 cups; set aside.
3. Heat butter and oil in large sauté pan over medium heat. Add half the potato slices and fry, turning with spatula, 2 to 3 minutes, or just until slices are evenly coated with fat and beginning to soften.
4. With slotted spatula, transfer fried potatoes to small shallow baking dish; reserve fat in pan. Season fried potatoes with salt and pepper and repeat with remaining potatoes, placing second batch on top of first when fried.
5. Bake potatoes, uncovered, about 20 minutes, or until fork-tender.
6. Remove potatoes from oven, cover loosely with foil, and keep warm on stove top until ready to serve.

Broiled Summer Squash and Tomatoes

2 small zucchini (about ¾ pound total weight)
2 small yellow squash (about ¾ pound total weight)
4 small tomatoes (about 1½ pounds total weight)
Small clove garlic
5 tablespoons unsalted butter
⅓ cup seasoned dry bread crumbs
Salt and freshly ground black pepper

1. Scrub zucchini and yellow squash under cold running water; rinse and dry with paper towels. Trim ends and discard. Halve each squash lengthwise; set aside.
2. Wash tomatoes and dry with paper towels. Cut ½-inch-thick slice from top of each tomato and, using sharp paring knife, cut around top in zigzag pattern; set tomatoes aside.
3. Peel and mince garlic; set aside.
4. Melt butter in small saucepan over low heat; set aside.
5. Preheat broiler.
6. Brush cut sides of squash halves with some of the

butter, place cut-side-down on broiler rack set 3 inches from heating element, and broil 5 minutes.
7. Turn squash and broil another 3 minutes.
8. Meanwhile, stir garlic, bread crumbs, and salt and pepper to taste into remaining butter.
9. Add tomatoes to broiler rack with squash, sprinkle all vegetables with crumb mixture, and broil another 2 minutes, or just until crumbs are golden brown.
10. Carefully transfer vegetables to platter. Cover loosely with foil and keep warm on stove top until ready to serve.

ADDED TOUCH

Profiteroles, or cream puffs, need not be intimidating to make. The pastry shells are foolproof if you do not overheat or overbeat the flour-butter mixture during its initial cooking; if cooked too long, the water that creates the steam for puffing evaporates.

Profiteroles

¼ cup sliced almonds (optional)
4 tablespoons unsalted butter
½ cup unsifted all-purpose flour
2 large eggs, at room temperature
½ cup heavy cream
½ cup semisweet chocolate chips
1 pint vanilla ice cream

1. Preheat oven to 350 degrees.
2. If using almonds, spread on baking sheet and toast in oven, shaking pan occasionally to prevent scorching, 5 to 8 minutes, or until light golden.
3. Meanwhile, heat butter and ½ cup water in small saucepan over medium heat until butter melts. Add flour all at once and stir vigorously with wooden spoon about 1 minute, or until mixture is well blended and forms a smooth ball. Remove from heat.
4. Remove almonds from oven and set aside to cool. Increase oven temperature to 400 degrees.
5. Add eggs to flour mixture, 1 at a time, beating after each addition until mixture is smooth.
6. Drop dough in 8 mounds, about 2 inches apart, onto ungreased cookie sheet and bake 20 to 25 minutes, or until puffed and golden brown.
7. Meanwhile, combine cream and chocolate chips in small heavy-gauge saucepan and bring to a boil over medium-low heat, stirring continuously with wooden spoon.
8. Reduce heat to low and cook another 2 to 3 minutes, stirring, or until mixture is slightly thickened.
9. Remove pan from heat and set mixture aside to cool to room temperature.
10. When done, transfer baked puffs to wire rack to cool.
11. Just before serving, cut tops off puffs and remove any uncooked dough from centers. Fill puffs with ice cream, replace tops, and place on platter, or divide among 4 dessert plates. Top each puff with chocolate sauce and sprinkle with toasted almond slices, if desired. Serve any remaining sauce separately.

"The Works" Whole-Wheat Pizza
Mixed Bean Salad

Whole-wheat pizza with a variety of toppings and a mixed bean salad make a quick, light supper just right for family or friends.

This no-yeast pizza crust has a quick-bread texture. After combining the dough ingredients, you roll out the dough right in the pizza pan; no tedious kneading or stretching is necessary. Use any or all of the toppings suggested here, or select others that your family might like better.

SHOPPING LIST AND STAPLES

4 ounces sliced pepperoni (approximately 16 slices)
½ pound green beans, or 1 pound if not using yellow (wax) beans
½ pound yellow (wax) beans, if available
¼ pound medium-size mushrooms
Small green bell pepper
Small red onion
15½-ounce jar spaghetti sauce
1-pound can red kidney beans
Large egg
¾ cup milk, approximately
8-ounce package mozzarëlla cheese
¼ cup plus 2 tablespoons vegetable oil
¼ cup olive oil
3 tablespoons red wine vinegar

1½ cups unsifted all-purpose flour, approximately
½ cup whole-wheat flour
2 tablespoons cornmeal
1 tablespoon baking powder
1½ tablespoons sugar, approximately
Salt
Freshly ground pepper

UTENSILS

Food processor (optional)
Medium-size skillet
Large saucepan
13- or 15-inch round pizza pan
2 large bowls
2 small bowls
Colander
Large strainer
Measuring cups and spoons
Chef's knife
Paring knife
Slotted spoon
Wooden spoon
Pizza wheel (optional)
Rolling pin
Grater (if not using processor)

START-TO-FINISH STEPS

1. Follow salad recipe steps 1 through 7.
2. Follow pizza recipe steps 1 through 14 and serve with salad.

RECIPES

"The Works" Whole-Wheat Pizza

2 tablespoons cornmeal
1¼ to 1½ cups unsifted all-purpose flour
½ cup whole-wheat flour
1 tablespoon baking powder
½ teaspoon salt
⅔ to ¾ cup milk
¼ cup plus 2 tablespoons vegetable oil
Large egg
8-ounce package mozzarella cheese
¼ pound medium-size mushrooms

1 cup spaghetti sauce
Small green bell pepper
16 slices pepperoni

1. Preheat oven to 450 degrees.
2. Grease 13- or 15-inch pizza pan and sprinkle bottom with cornmeal. Tilt and rotate pan until evenly coated; discard excess.
3. In large bowl, combine 1¼ cups all-purpose flour, whole-wheat flour, baking powder, and salt, and stir with fork to blend; set aside.
4. Combine ⅔ cup milk, ¼ cup oil, and egg in small bowl and stir with fork until well blended.
5. Stirring with wooden spoon, gradually add milk mixture to dry ingredients and stir until a soft, moist dough forms. If dough is too sticky to gather into a ball, gradually add more flour; if too dry, add more milk.
6. Turn dough onto prepared pan and flatten to 1-inch thickness. Cover dough with sheet of waxed paper and, with rolling pin, roll out dough to ¼-inch thickness. Remove waxed paper and, with floured fingertips, pinch dough around edge to form ½-inch raised rim. Bake pizza crust 15 minutes, or until lightly browned.
7. Meanwhile, in food processor fitted with shredding disk, or with grater, shred cheese; set aside.
8. Wipe mushrooms clean with damp paper towels. Trim stems and discard. Cut enough mushrooms into ⅛-inch-thick slices to measure 1 cup; set aside. Line plate with double thickness of paper towels.
9. Heat remaining 2 tablespoons oil in medium-size skillet over medium-high heat. Add mushrooms and sauté, stirring, 1 minute, or just until wilted.
10. With slotted spoon, transfer mushrooms to paper-towel-lined plate to drain; set aside.
11. Remove crust from oven and sprinkle with half the cheese. Spoon spaghetti sauce over cheese and, with back of spoon, spread evenly over crust. Top with remaining cheese and sprinkle with mushrooms. Bake pizza another 10 to 15 minutes, or until crust is browned and cheese is bubbly.
12. Meanwhile, wash, core and seed green pepper. Cut lengthwise into at least 16 strips; set aside.
13. Remove pizza from oven. Top with pepper strips and pepperoni, and return to oven for a few minutes to warm pepperoni and peppers.
14. Remove pizza from oven and cut into 8 wedges. Divide among 4 dinner plates and serve.

Mixed Bean Salad

½ pound green beans, or 1 pound if not using yellow
  (wax) beans
½ pound yellow (wax) beans, if available
Small red onion
1-pound can red kidney beans
¼ cup olive oil
3 tablespoons red wine vinegar
¾ teaspoon salt
Pinch of freshly ground pepper
1 to 1½ tablespoons sugar

1. Bring 2 quarts water to a boil in large saucepan.
2. Meanwhile, trim stem ends of fresh beans. Cut beans crosswise into 1-inch pieces and add to boiling water. After water returns to a boil, cook beans, uncovered, 1 to 2 minutes, or until crisp-tender.
3. Transfer beans to colander, refresh under cold running water, and set aside to drain.
4. Peel onion and cut crosswise into ⅛-inch-thick slices.
5. Rinse kidney beans in large strainer; drain thoroughly.
6. Combine all the beans and the onion slices in large bowl and toss to combine; set aside.
7. For dressing, combine oil, vinegar, salt, pepper, and sugar to taste in small bowl, and beat with fork until blended. Pour dressing over beans and toss until evenly coated. Cover and refrigerate until ready to serve.

ADDED TOUCHES

For a smooth and thick custard sauce, use a heavy-gauge saucepan to assure even heat distribution.

Fresh Fruit Cup with Custard Sauce

1 pint strawberries
1 cup seedless green grapes
1 lemon
Small banana
Custard Sauce (see following recipe)

1. Rinse, dry, and hull strawberries. Cut any very large berries into pieces.
2. Wash and dry grapes. Halve lengthwise; set aside.
3. Squeeze enough lemon juice to measure 1 tablespoon.
4. Peel banana and cut crosswise into 1-inch pieces. Place banana in small bowl and sprinkle with lemon juice to prevent discoloration; toss gently until evenly coated.

5. Divide fruit among 4 small bowls or cups, top with custard sauce, and serve.

Custard Sauce

½ cup milk
2 egg yolks, at room temperature
2 tablespoons sugar
2 tablespoons Marsala, or ½ teaspoon vanilla extract

1. Heat milk in small heavy-gauge nonaluminum saucepan over low heat about 3 minutes, or just until small bubbles appear around edge of pan.
2. Meanwhile, combine egg yolks and sugar in small bowl and beat with electric hand mixer at high speed 1 to 2 minutes, or until light and fluffy.
3. Beating at low speed, gradually add scalded milk and beat until totally incorporated.
4. Return mixture to saucepan and cook over low heat, beating continuously with hand mixer at low speed, 2 to 3 minutes, or until custard thickens slightly. Simmer sauce 1 minute.
5. Add Marsala or vanilla extract and beat at medium speed 5 minutes, or until mixture holds its shape slightly when dropped from a spoon; do *not* overcook.
6. Remove pan from heat and cover until ready to serve.

Amaretti, Italian almond macaroons, are the perfect accompaniment for fruit desserts.

Amaretti

7-ounce roll almond paste
2 egg whites
¼ teaspoon almond extract
½ cup granulated sugar
4-ounce can natural almond slices for garnish (optional)

1. Preheat oven to 300 degrees.
2. Line 2 cookie sheets with parchment paper or foil.
3. Crumble almond paste into small bowl. Add egg whites and almond extract, and beat with electric mixer at medium speed 3 minutes, or until well blended.
4. Still beating, add sugar slowly and beat until smooth.
5. Drop dough by rounded teaspoons, about 2 inches apart, onto cookie sheets. You will have about 2½ dozen cookies. Garnish each with an almond slice, if desired, and bake 20 minutes, or until firm and lightly browned.
6. Transfer paper or foil with amaretti to racks to cool.
7. Peel off paper, transfer amaretti to platter, and serve.

Jane Kirby

MENU 1 (Left)
Cheese and Prosciutto Calzoni
Green Beans and Onions Vinaigrette
Carrots with Orange-Honey Dressing

MENU 2
Pork Chops with Orange Sauce
Bulgur Pilaf
Peas with Mint

MENU 3
Honey-Lime Chicken Breasts
Corn with Peppers and Onion
Cheddar Drop Biscuits

As a dietitian, Jane Kirby is committed to serving wholesome meals, but she is not an advocate of health foods, megavitamins, or nutritional fads. She believes that people are best nourished by eating a wide variety of foods and that there are no such things as "kids' foods" and "adults' foods." At her house, even French fries and banana splits are allowed because they are part of good square meals. All three of her menus are planned not only for nutritional balance but also for flavor and appearance.

Neapolitan *calzoni*, or pizza turnovers, filled with a blend of three mild cheeses and prosciutto, are the fun-to-eat main course of Menu 1. This easy-to-prepare meal also features green beans vinaigrette and carrots with a honey and orange dressing.

Menu 2 offers meaty loin pork chops, which the cook skillet-braises for about half an hour in orange juice spiced with cloves. The chops are accompanied by a bulgur pilaf flecked with orange peel, raisins, and almonds, and by peas flavored with garlic and mint.

Menu 3 is another delicious meal that the whole family will ask for time and again. Boned and skinned chicken breasts are quickly sautéed, then topped with a subtle honey-lime sauce. With the chicken, Jane Kirby serves corn mixed with bell peppers and onion, and tasty buttermilk-Cheddar biscuits.

Golden calzoni *filled with cheese and prosciutto go well with two vegetable salads—carrots with orange zest, and green beans and onions vinaigrette. Iced tea garnished with lemon slices is refreshing with this meal.*

47

Cheese and Prosciutto Calzoni
Green Beans and Onions Vinaigrette
Carrots with Orange-Honey Dressing

Portable pizzas, *calzoni* are perfect for cook-outs as well as for casual indoor suppers: Just reheat them over the coals as you would in the oven. The *calzoni* filling is made with mozzarella, ricotta, and Parmesan cheese mixed with prosciutto, a dry-cured unsmoked ham with a dark pink color and mild flavor. Prosciutto is available at most supermarkets and Italian groceries.

SHOPPING LIST AND STAPLES

2 ounces prosciutto or baked ham
1 pound green beans
1 pound baby carrots or medium-size carrots
Medium-size yellow or white onion
Small red onion
1 bunch parsley
Medium-size orange
8¼-ounce can whole tomatoes
8-ounce package mozzarella cheese
8-ounce container ricotta cheese
2 ounces Parmesan cheese
1-pound loaf frozen bread dough
1 cup olive or vegetable oil, approximately
⅓ cup cider vinegar
1 tablespoon Dijon mustard
2 tablespoons honey
2 tablespoons all-purpose flour, approximately
1 teaspoon dried oregano
Salt and freshly ground black pepper

UTENSILS

Food processor (optional)
Steamer unit or saucepan large enough to accommodate
   collapsible steamer, with cover
Collapsible steamer (if not using steamer unit)
17 x 11-inch baking sheet
3 medium-size bowls, one nonaluminum
Small bowl
Colander
Strainer
Measuring cups and spoons
Chef's knife
Paring knife
Slotted spoon
Metal spatula
Pastry brush

Small jar with tight-fitting lid
Grater
Citrus juicer
Rolling pin

START-TO-FINISH STEPS

Four hours ahead: Set out frozen bread dough to thaw for calzoni recipe.

1. Follow beans and onions recipe steps 1 through 4.
2. Wash parsley and dry with paper towels. Trim ends and discard. Mince enough parsley to measure 2 tablespoons for calzoni recipe and 3 tablespoons for beans and onions recipe. Reserve remainder for another use.
3. Follow beans and onions recipe steps 5 and 6.
4. Follow carrots recipe steps 1 through 6.
5. Follow calzoni recipe steps 1 through 10, beans and onions recipe step 7, carrots recipe step 7, and serve.

RECIPES

Cheese and Prosciutto Calzoni

8¼-ounce can whole tomatoes
8-ounce package mozzarella cheese
2 ounces Parmesan cheese
2 ounces prosciutto or baked ham
Small red onion
8-ounce container ricotta cheese
2 tablespoons minced fresh parsley
Freshly ground black pepper
2 tablespoons all-purpose flour, approximately
1-pound loaf frozen bread dough, thawed
1 tablespoon olive or vegetable oil, approximately
1 teaspoon dried oregano

1. Turn tomatoes into strainer set over small bowl and drain well; reserve liquid for another use. Gently squeeze tomatoes to remove seeds. Chop tomatoes; set aside.
2. Halve mozzarella crosswise. Using food processor fitted with shredding disk, or coarse side of grater, shred one half of mozzarella; reserve remaining half for another use.
3. Using grater, grate enough Parmesan cheese to measure 2 tablespoons; set aside.
4. With chef's knife, finely chop prosciutto or ham.
5. Halve and peel onion. Mince enough onion to measure ¼ cup; set aside. Reserve remaining onion for another use.

6. For filling, combine tomatoes, mozzarella, Parmesan, ham, onion, ricotta, parsley, and pepper to taste in medium-size bowl and stir with fork to blend. You should have about 2 cups filling.

7. Preheat oven to 400 degrees.

8. On floured surface, roll out one-quarter of dough into ¼- to ½-inch-thick 6-inch round with lightly floured rolling pin. Spoon one-quarter of filling onto one side of the dough, leaving a 1-inch border around edge. Moisten edge with water, fold dough over filling so that edges meet, and press to seal; transfer to ungreased baking sheet. Repeat with remaining dough and filling, making 4 calzoni in all.

9. Bake calzoni 15 to 18 minutes, or until golden.

10. Remove baked calzoni from oven, brush each with oil, and sprinkle with oregano. With metal spatula, transfer calzoni to 4 dinner plates and serve.

Green Beans and Onions Vinaigrette

1 pound green beans
Medium-size yellow or white onion

Dressing:
½ cup olive or vegetable oil
⅓ cup cider vinegar
1 tablespoon Dijon mustard
3 tablespoons minced fresh parsley
¼ teaspoon salt
Pinch of freshly ground black pepper

1. Trim ends from beans. Place beans in colander and rinse under cold running water; set aside.

2. Peel onion and cut crosswise into ¼-inch-thick slices. Separate into rings; set aside.

3. Fill bottom of steamer unit, or saucepan large enough to accommodate collapsible steamer, with enough cold water to come up to but not over steamer basket and bring to a boil over high heat.

4. Add beans and onions to steamer, cover pan, and steam about 6 minutes, or until vegetables are crisp-tender.

5. Turn vegetables into colander and refresh under cold running water. Drain well and dry with paper towels. Place vegetables in medium-size nonaluminum bowl.

6. Combine dressing ingredients in small jar with lid and shake until well blended. Pour over vegetables and toss until evenly coated; set aside until ready to serve.

7. Using slotted spoon, divide green beans and onions among dinner plates and serve.

Carrots with Orange-Honey Dressing

1 pound baby carrots or medium-size carrots
Medium-size orange
⅓ cup olive or vegetable oil
2 tablespoons honey
½ teaspoon salt
Pinch of freshly ground black pepper

1. Peel and trim carrots. If using medium-size carrots, cut crosswise into thirds, then halve pieces lengthwise.

2. Fill steamer unit, or saucepan large enough to accommodate collapsible steamer, with enough cold water to come up to but not over steamer basket and bring to a boil over high heat.

3. Add carrots to steamer and cook about 8 minutes, or until crisp-tender.

4. Meanwhile, wash and dry orange. Using grater, grate enough rind to measure 1 tablespoon, then squeeze enough juice to measure ½ cup; set both aside.

5. Turn carrots into colander and refresh under cold running water. Drain and dry with paper towels. Place carrots in medium-size nonaluminum bowl.

6. In small jar with tight-fitting lid, combine grated orange rind, orange juice, and remaining ingredients, and shake until well blended. Pour over carrots and toss until evenly coated; set aside until ready to serve.

7. Using slotted spoon, divide carrots among dinner plates and serve.

ADDED TOUCH

These delicate, spicy cookies will be a welcome addition to the family cookie jar.

Chocolate-Cinnamon Wafers

2½ cups all-purpose flour
2 teaspoons baking powder
1½ teaspoons cinnamon
½ teaspoon salt
1 stick unsalted butter or margarine,
   at room temperature
1¼ cups granulated sugar
2 eggs, at room temperature
1 teaspoon vanilla extract
½ cup unsweetened cocoa powder

1. Combine flour, baking powder, cinnamon, and salt in medium-size bowl, and stir with fork until well blended.

2. Combine butter and sugar in another medium-size bowl and beat with electric mixer at medium speed until fluffy.

3. One at a time, add eggs, beating after each addition until totally incorporated.

4. Add vanilla and continue beating, occasionally scraping down sides of bowl with rubber spatula, until mixture is light and fluffy.

5. Stir in cocoa, then gradually add other dry ingredients, stirring until well blended.

6. Shape dough into ball, wrap in waxed paper, and refrigerate for several hours, or until firm and easy to handle.

7. Preheat oven to 375 degrees.

8. Place about one-fifth of dough directly on ungreased cookie sheet and roll out to about ¹⁄₁₆-inch thickness with lightly floured rolling pin. Using 2½-inch cookie cutter, cut out cookies, leaving about 1 inch between them. Remove dough between cookies and bake cookies 8 to 10 minutes.

9. Transfer cookies to wire rack to cool completely.

10. Recombine dough scraps and repeat with remaining dough, rechilling dough, if necessary, for easier handling. You will have about 7½ dozen cookies.

Pork Chops with Orange Sauce
Bulgur Pilaf
Peas with Mint

The flavors of orange and mint predominate in this simple dinner of braised pork chops with orange sauce, bulgur with raisins, almonds, and orange zest, and peas with mint. For an appealing garnish, twist an orange slice into an S shape.

For this meal, bulgur pilaf is served as an accompaniment to the pork. Sometimes mistakenly called cracked wheat, bulgur is whole-wheat berries that are steam-cooked, dried, and then ground.

SHOPPING LIST AND STAPLES

Four 1-inch-thick loin pork chops (about 1¾ pounds total weight)
2 small cloves garlic
Small bunch fresh parsley
Small bunch fresh mint, or 2 teaspoons dried
2 juice oranges
Medium-size navel orange (optional)
2 cups chicken stock, preferably homemade (see page 12), or canned
4 tablespoons unsalted butter or margarine
16-ounce bag frozen peas
1 cup bulgur
15-ounce package dark or golden raisins
2½-ounce package slivered almonds
1 teaspoon sugar
½ teaspoon cornstarch
1 teaspoon whole cloves
Salt and freshly ground pepper

UTENSILS

Large heavy-gauge skillet with cover
Medium-size skillet
Medium-size saucepan with cover
Heatproof platter
2 medium-size heatproof bowls
Measuring cups and spoons
Chef's knife
Paring knife
Wooden spoon
Slotted spoon
Whisk
Metal tongs
Grater
Citrus juicer

START-TO-FINISH STEPS

One hour ahead: Set out frozen peas to thaw.

1. Wash 1 juice orange and dry with paper towel. Using

grater, grate enough rind, avoiding white pith as much as possible, to measure 1 tablespoon for pilaf recipe. Squeeze enough juice from juice oranges to measure ¾ cup for pork chops recipe.
2. Follow pork chops recipe steps 1 through 6.
3. Follow pilaf recipe steps 1 through 4.
4. Follow peas recipe steps 1 through 6.
5. Follow pork chops recipe steps 7 and 8.
6. Follow pilaf recipe steps 5 and 6.
7. Follow pork chops recipe steps 9 and 10 and serve with pilaf and peas.

RECIPES

Pork Chops with Orange Sauce

Four 1-inch-thick loin pork chops (about 1¾ pounds total weight)
¾ cup freshly squeezed orange juice
1 teaspoon sugar
1 teaspoon salt
1 teaspoon whole cloves
½ teaspoon cornstarch
Medium-size navel orange for garnish (optional)

1. Trim excess fat from pork chops; reserve fat.
2. Place large heavy-gauge skillet over medium-high heat and run pork fat over bottom to grease it; discard fat.
3. Add chops; cook 4 minutes per side, or until browned.
4. Add orange juice, sugar, salt, and cloves to skillet, increase heat to high, and bring to a boil. Reduce heat to low, cover, and simmer 25 to 30 minutes, or until chops are fork-tender.
5. Meanwhile, combine cornstarch and 2 tablespoons water in measuring cup and stir until cornstarch dissolves.
6. Wash and dry navel orange, if using. Cut four ¼-inch-thick slices crosswise from orange.
7. Transfer chops to heatproof platter and keep warm in 200-degree oven.
8. Spoon off fat from skillet. Boil remaining liquid over high heat about 10 minutes, or until reduced by half.
9. Add cornstarch mixture to liquid in skillet and whisk until blended. Continue to cook, whisking constantly, about 1 minute, or until sauce is thickened. Remove cloves and reserve for garnish, if desired.
10. Divide pork chops among 4 dinner plates, top with sauce, and garnish each serving with a slice of orange and some cloves, if desired.

Bulgur Pilaf

3 tablespoons unsalted butter or margarine
½ cup slivered almonds
1 cup bulgur
2 cups chicken stock
Small bunch parsley
1 cup dark or golden raisins
1 tablespoon grated orange rind

1. Line plate with double thickness of paper towels.
2. Heat butter or margarine in medium-size saucepan over medium heat. Add almonds and sauté, stirring, 2 minutes, or just until golden. With slotted spoon, transfer almonds to paper-towel-lined plate; set aside to drain.
3. Add bulgur to butter or margarine remaining in saucepan and sauté, stirring, 1 minute, or just until well coated.
4. Stir in stock and bring to a boil over high heat. Reduce heat to low, cover, and simmer, undisturbed, 25 to 30 minutes, or until liquid is totally absorbed.
5. Wash parsley and dry with paper towels. Trim stem ends and discard. Mince enough parsley to measure ⅓ cup; reserve remainder for another use.
6. Add almonds, parsley, raisins, and orange rind to bulgur and toss gently to combine. Turn into ovenproof bowl and keep warm in 200-degree oven until ready to serve.

Peas with Mint

Small bunch fresh mint, or 2 teaspoons dried
2 small cloves garlic
1 tablespoon unsalted butter or margarine
16-ounce bag frozen peas, thawed
¼ teaspoon salt
Pinch of freshly ground pepper

1. Preheat oven to 200 degrees.
2. Wash fresh mint, if using, and pat dry with paper towels. Mince enough mint leaves to measure ¼ cup; set aside. Reserve remainder for another use.
3. Peel and mince enough garlic to measure 2 teaspoons.
4. Heat butter or margarine in medium-size skillet over medium heat. Add garlic and sauté, stirring occasionally, 1 minute, or until transparent; do *not* brown.
5. Add peas, mint, salt, and pepper to pan, and cook, stirring gently, about 5 minutes, or until heated through.
6. Turn peas into heatproof bowl, cover loosely with foil, and keep warm in oven until ready to serve.

Honey-Lime Chicken Breasts
Corn with Peppers and Onion
Cheddar Drop Biscuits

Sit your family down to a tempting meal of chicken breasts with honey-lime sauce, corn with diced peppers and onion, and warm Cheddar cheese biscuits. Serve extra biscuits in a napkin-lined basket.

Flattening the chicken breasts before cooking ensures that they cook through quickly. Pound them from the center outward, so each breast is of even thickness.

SHOPPING LIST AND STAPLES

2 whole boneless, skinless chicken breasts, halved (about 1 pound total weight)
1 each medium-size red and green bell pepper
Small avocado (optional)
Small onion
Small bunch parsley
1 lemon (if using avocado)
2 large limes
¾ cup chicken stock, preferably homemade (see page 12), or canned
6 tablespoons unsalted butter
1 cup buttermilk
¼ pound Cheddar cheese
10-ounce package frozen corn kernels
¼ cup olive or vegetable oil
⅔ cup honey
2¼ cups all-purpose flour, approximately
2 teaspoons baking powder
¼ teaspoon baking soda
½ teaspoon dried thyme
Cayenne pepper
Salt

UTENSILS

Large heavy-gauge skillet with cover
Medium-size heavy-gauge skillet
17 x 11-inch baking sheet
Heatproof platter
9-inch pie plate
2 medium-size bowls, one heatproof
Small nonaluminum bowl
Strainer
Measuring cups and spoons
Chef's knife
Paring knife
Wooden spoon
Metal spatula
Pastry blender or 2 knives
Metal tongs
Grater or zester
Meat mallet or rolling pin

START-TO-FINISH STEPS

One hour ahead: Set out corn to thaw.

1. Follow biscuits recipe steps 1 through 7.
2. Follow corn recipe steps 1 and 2.
3. Follow biscuits recipe step 8, reduce oven temperature to 200 degrees, and follow corn recipe steps 3 through 7.
4. Follow chicken recipe steps 1 through 6.
5. While chicken cooks, follow biscuits recipe step 9.
6. Follow chicken recipe steps 7 through 10, corn recipe step 8, and serve with biscuits.

RECIPES

Honey-Lime Chicken Breasts

2 large limes
¼ cup all-purpose flour, approximately
2 whole boneless, skinless chicken breasts, halved (about 1 pound total weight)
2 tablespoons unsalted butter
2 tablespoons olive or vegetable oil
¾ cup chicken stock
⅔ cup honey
¼ teaspoon salt
Pinch of Cayenne pepper

1. Wash one lime and dry with paper towel. Using grater or zester, grate rind from lime, avoiding white pith as much as possible; set aside. Squeeze enough juice from peeled lime plus second lime to measure ¼ cup; set juice aside.
2. Place flour in pie plate; set aside.
3. Wash and dry chicken. Place each chicken breast half between two sheets of waxed paper and pound to ⅛-inch thickness with meat mallet or rolling pin.
4. Heat butter and oil in large heavy-gauge skillet over medium-high heat.
5. Working quickly, dredge each breast half in flour, gently shake off excess, and add to hot fat in skillet. Sauté breasts 3 minutes per side, or until browned.
6. Add stock to skillet and bring to a boil. Reduce heat to low, cover, and simmer 3 to 5 minutes, or until breasts are fork-tender.
7. Transfer chicken breasts to heatproof platter, cover loosely with foil, and keep warm in 200-degree oven.
8. For sauce, add honey, grated rind, salt, and Cayenne pepper to liquid in skillet and stir until blended. Increase heat to high, bring to a rapid boil, and boil 5 to 7 minutes, or until sauce is reduced and slightly thickened.
9. Add lime juice to sauce and stir until blended; remove skillet from heat.
10. Divide chicken breasts among 4 dinner plates and top with equal portions of sauce.

Corn with Peppers and Onion

Medium-size red bell pepper
Medium-size green bell pepper
Small onion
2 tablespoons olive or vegetable oil
Small bunch parsley
1 lemon (if using avocado)
Small avocado (optional)
10-ounce package frozen corn kernels, thawed and drained
¼ teaspoon salt

1. Wash and dry bell peppers. Halve, core, and seed. Coarsely chop enough peppers to measure 1½ cups total.
2. Peel onion and cut crosswise into thin slices.
3. Heat oil in medium-size heavy-gauge skillet over medium heat. Add peppers and onion, and sauté, stirring occasionally, about 10 minutes, or until tender but not browned.
4. Meanwhile, wash and dry parsley. Trim stem ends and discard. Chop enough parsley to measure ⅓ cup; set aside. Reserve remainder for another use.
5. If using avocado, squeeze enough lemon juice to measure 2 tablespoons; set aside.
6. Halve avocado lengthwise, cutting around and under pit. Twist halves in opposite directions to separate. Remove and discard pit. Peel avocado, cut into ½-inch dice, and place in small bowl. Sprinkle with lemon juice to prevent discoloration and toss gently until evenly coated.
7. Add corn and salt to vegetables in skillet and stir to combine. Turn vegetables into medium-size heatproof bowl, cover with foil, and keep warm in 200-degree oven.
8. Just before serving, fold in parsley and avocado. Divide among 4 dinner plates and serve.

Cheddar Drop Biscuits

¼ pound Cheddar cheese
4 tablespoons unsalted butter, well chilled
2 cups all-purpose flour
2 teaspoons baking powder
¼ teaspoon baking soda
½ teaspoon salt
½ teaspoon dried thyme
1 cup buttermilk

1. Preheat oven to 450 degrees.
2. Using grater, shred enough Cheddar to measure ¾ cup; set aside.
3. Cut butter into 1-tablespoon pieces; set aside.
4. Combine flour, baking powder, baking soda, salt, and thyme in medium-size bowl and stir with fork to blend.
5. Using pastry blender or 2 knives, cut in butter until mixture resembles coarse cornmeal.
6. With wooden spoon, stir in buttermilk and ½ cup shredded Cheddar, and beat vigorously 30 seconds.
7. Drop batter by heaping tablespoonful at least 2 inches apart onto ungreased baking sheet, making 10 to 12 biscuits. Sprinkle each biscuit with remaining Cheddar and bake 8 to 10 minutes, or until puffed and golden.
8. Transfer biscuits to wire cooling racks.
9. A few minutes before serving, wrap biscuits loosely in foil and place in oven to warm, if desired.

Nina Simonds

Nina Simonds, who has earned her culinary reputation as an expert chef and teacher of Chinese cooking, can easily make the transition to other cuisines as well. She finds this a particularly valuable skill when planning family menus. "Serving food from a number of different countries," she says, "is an ideal way to introduce children to unusual ingredients and dishes." The three menus she offers here demonstrate her eclectic approach to home cooking.

Poultry is one of Nina Simonds's favorite meats because it is generally lean, high in protein, and adaptable to a variety of seasonings and cooking methods. For Menu 1, a Mediterranean-style meal, she selects turkey breast meat, which she cubes and then marinates on skewers with mushrooms and peppers for kabobs. With the kabobs she provides a colorful rice and vegetable salad.

Chicken drumsticks—ideal finger food for children— are the focus of her country-French Menu 2. She serves the chicken with two tempting vegetable dishes: broccoli sautéed with bacon, and carrots coated with a honey-lemon glaze.

Chinese flavors mingle in Menu 3, in which Cornish game hens are marinated in a *hoisin*-based sauce for the entrée. Snow peas and almonds stir fried with sesame oil, and a salad of bean sprouts and red pepper strips in a soy sauce and rice vinegar dressing are the Oriental accompaniments.

Broil cubed turkey, mushrooms, and green peppers on fanciful skewers for a delicious family meal. The bold linens and dinnerware pick up the colors of the rice and vegetable salad.

Turkey, Pepper, and Mushroom Kabobs
Chilled Rice and Vegetable Salad

Packaged turkey breast is readily available fresh or frozen at most supermarkets. Even though turkey breast is fairly tender, marinating it tenderizes the meat further and adds flavor. Heating the marinade helps it to penetrate the meat cubes more rapidly.

A chilled rice and vegetable salad sparked with a pungent dressing is a flavorful complement to the turkey kabobs. Be sure to chill the cooked rice before assembling the salad so that the grains do not stick together.

If you are serving the kabobs to small children, you may want to remove the turkey, peppers, and mushrooms from the skewers once cooked.

SHOPPING LIST AND STAPLES

½ boneless turkey breast (about 1½ pounds)
2 ripe avocados
½ pound button mushrooms
2 medium-size tomatoes (about 1 pound total weight)
2 medium-size green bell peppers (about ½ pound total weight)
Medium-size red onion
2 cloves garlic
Small bunch fresh parsley
Small bunch fresh basil, or ½ teaspoon dried
Small bunch fresh oregano, or 1 teaspoon dried
1 lemon (optional)
1¼ cups olive oil
¼ cup safflower or corn oil
¼ cup plus 2 tablespoons red wine vinegar
1 teaspoon Dijon mustard
1½ cups long-grain rice
Salt
Freshly ground black pepper
½ cup dry red wine

UTENSILS

Medium-size heavy-gauge saucepan with cover
Small nonaluminum saucepan
9 x 12-inch shallow flameproof glass or ceramic baking dish
Jelly-roll pan
Large bowl
Small nonaluminum bowl
Measuring cups and spoons
Chef's knife

Paring knife
Wooden spoon
Wire whisk
Eight 12-inch stainless steel or bamboo skewers

START-TO-FINISH STEPS

1. Follow rice salad recipe step 1 and kabobs recipe step 1.
2. Follow rice salad recipe step 2.
3. While rice simmers, wash parsley, and fresh basil and oregano if using; pat dry with paper towels. Trim stem ends and discard. Chop enough parsley to measure 2 tablespoons for rice salad recipe. Set aside 4 basil sprigs for garnish, if using, and chop enough basil leaves to measure 1 teaspoon for kabobs recipe. Chop enough oregano to measure 2 teaspoons for kabobs recipe. Reserve remaining herbs for another use.
4. Follow kabobs recipe steps 2 through 4.
5. Follow rice salad recipe step 3 and kabobs recipe steps 5 through 9.
6. Follow rice salad recipe steps 4 through 6 and kabobs recipe step 10.
7. Follow rice salad recipe steps 7 through 9.
8. Follow kabobs recipe steps 11 through 14 and serve with rice salad.

RECIPES

Turkey, Pepper, and Mushroom Kabobs

Marinade:
2 cloves garlic
1 cup olive oil
½ cup dry red wine
2 tablespoons red wine vinegar
1 teaspoon salt
2 teaspoons chopped fresh oregano, or 1 teaspoon dried
1 teaspoon chopped fresh basil, or ½ teaspoon dried
½ teaspoon freshly ground black pepper

½ pound button mushrooms
2 medium-size green bell peppers (about ½ pound total weight)
½ boneless turkey breast (about 1½ pounds)

Garnishes (optional):
1 lemon
4 sprigs fresh basil

1. If using bamboo skewers, place 8 in a 9 x 12-inch shallow flameproof glass or ceramic baking dish, add enough cold water to cover, and set aside to soak.

2. Bruise garlic under flat blade of chef's knife; remove and discard peels.

3. In small nonaluminum saucepan, combine marinade ingredients and bring to a boil over high heat. Reduce heat to medium and simmer 5 minutes.

4. Remove marinade from heat and set aside to cool.

5. Wipe mushrooms clean with damp paper towels. Trim stem ends and discard. Set aside.

6. Wash peppers and dry with paper towels. Halve, core, and seed peppers. Cut into 1½-inch squares; set aside.

7. Remove and discard skin and any cartilage from turkey breast. Cut breast into 1½-inch cubes; set aside.

8. Remove skewers from water, if necessary, and dry baking dish. Thread turkey cubes, green pepper squares, and mushrooms alternately on 8 skewers and place kabobs in baking dish.

9. Pour marinade over kabobs and turn to coat. Set aside to marinate at room temperature at least 15 minutes, turning every 5 minutes.

10. Preheat broiler.

11. Place baking dish with kabobs and marinade 3 to 4 inches from heating element and broil kabobs 12 to 15 minutes on one side, basting if desired, until turkey is brown.

12. Turn skewers and broil another 12 to 15 minutes, basting if desired.

13. Wash lemon, if using, and dry with paper towel. Cut four ¼-inch-thick slices; set aside.

14. Place 2 skewers on each of 4 dinner plates and garnish each serving with a slice of lemon and a sprig of basil, if desired.

Chilled Rice and Vegetable Salad

1½ cups long-grain rice
2 medium-size tomatoes (about 1 pound total weight)
2 ripe avocados
Medium-size red onion
2 tablespoons minced parsley

Dressing:
¼ cup olive oil
¼ cup safflower or corn oil
¼ cup red wine vinegar
1 teaspoon Dijon mustard
1¼ teaspoons salt
¼ teaspoon freshly ground black pepper

1. Bring 3 cups water to a boil in medium-size heavy-gauge saucepan over high heat.

2. Stir rice into boiling water. Cover pan, reduce heat to medium-low, and simmer gently, undisturbed, 18 to 20 minutes, or until water is completely absorbed.

3. Fluff rice with fork and transfer to jelly-roll pan. Spread out rice evenly in pan, cover with plastic wrap, and place in freezer to chill.

4. Wash tomatoes and dry with paper towels. Core and halve each tomato crosswise. Gently squeeze each half to remove seeds. Cut tomatoes into ½-inch cubes; set aside. You should have about 2 cups cubes.

5. Halve each avocado lengthwise, cutting around pit. Twist halves in opposite directions to separate; remove and discard pits. Peel avocados and cut into ½-inch cubes; set aside. You should have about 3 cups cubes.

6. Halve, peel, and coarsely dice enough onion to measure 1 cup; set aside.

7. Combine chilled rice, tomatoes, avocados, onion, and parsley in large bowl and toss gently to combine.

8. Combine dressing ingredients in small nonaluminum bowl and whisk vigorously until well blended.

9. Pour dressing over rice salad and toss gently until evenly coated. Cover with plastic wrap and refrigerate until ready to serve.

ADDED TOUCH

Choose slightly underripe bananas for this elegant fruit dessert. If the bananas are overripe, they will be too pulpy after baking and will lose their shape.

Baked Bananas with Shaved Chocolate

4 tablespoons unsalted butter
1 lemon
4 slightly underripe bananas
½ cup granulated sugar
½ cup Grand Marnier or other orange-flavored liqueur (optional)
4 tablespoons sweet dark chocolate shavings

1. Preheat oven to 400 degrees.

2. In small saucepan, melt butter over low heat.

3. Meanwhile, squeeze enough lemon juice to measure 2 tablespoons; set aside.

4. Cut four 12-inch-square sheets of foil and brush dull side of each generously with melted butter.

5. Peel and halve bananas lengthwise. Place a pair of halves, cut-sides-up, in center of 1 foil square. Sprinkle bananas with lemon juice, sugar, and Grand Marnier if using, and reassemble halves. Turn bananas on diagonal in center of foil squares, fold foil to form triangle, and seal edges.

6. Transfer foil packets to baking sheet and bake bananas 8 to 10 minutes, or until fragrant.

7. Transfer packets to dessert plates and cut foil open. Sprinkle each serving with shaved chocolate and serve.

Chicken Drumsticks with Tarragon-Shallot Butter
Sautéed Broccoli with Bacon and Onion
Glazed Carrots

For a casual buffet, offer chicken drumsticks arranged around sautéed broccoli, and a second platter of glazed carrots.

Choose meaty drumsticks so that two per person will be a substantial entrée. The drumsticks are enriched with tarragon, shallots, and butter stuffed into a pocket made by slitting one side of the drumstick. As the chicken cooks, the butter and seasonings permeate and moisten the meat.

8 meaty chicken drumsticks (about 2 pounds total weight)
¼ pound sliced bacon
4 large carrots (about 1 pound total weight), or 1 pound baby carrots
1 bunch broccoli (about 1¼ pounds)
Medium-size yellow onion
2 shallots
Small bunch fresh parsley
Small bunch fresh tarragon, or 1 tablespoon dried
1 lemon
½ cup chicken stock, preferably homemade (see page 12), or canned
Large egg
½ pint heavy cream
6 tablespoons unsalted butter
3 tablespoons safflower or corn oil
1 tablespoon honey
Salt
Freshly ground black pepper
½ cup dry white wine

UTENSILS

Large heavy-gauge skillet or sauté pan with cover
Medium-size heavy-gauge skillet or sauté pan with cover
Medium-size saucepan with cover
3 medium-size heatproof serving platters
Small bowl
Measuring cups and spoons
Chef's knife
Paring knife
Wooden spoon
Whisk
Metal tongs
Vegetable peeler

START-TO-FINISH STEPS

1. Prepare herbs for drumsticks and carrot recipes. Reserve remaining herbs for another use.
2. Follow drumsticks recipe steps 1 through 5.
3. While drumsticks are browning, follow broccoli recipe steps 1 through 3.
4. Follow drumsticks recipe step 6.
5. Follow carrots recipe steps 1 through 4.
6. While carrots simmer, follow broccoli recipe steps 4 through 7.
7. Follow carrots recipe step 5, drumsticks recipe step 7, and broccoli recipe step 8.
8. Follow drumsticks recipe steps 8 through 12, carrots recipe step 6, and serve with broccoli.

RECIPES

Chicken Drumsticks with Tarragon-Shallot Butter

2 shallots
2 tablespoons chopped fresh tarragon, or 1 tablespoon dried
1 teaspoon salt
½ teaspoon freshly ground black pepper
4 tablespoons unsalted butter
8 meaty chicken drumsticks (about 2 pounds total weight)
3 tablespoons safflower or corn oil
½ cup dry white wine
Large egg
¾ cup heavy cream
1 tablespoon chopped fresh parsley for garnish

1. Peel and mince enough shallots to measure 1 tablespoon.
2. Combine shallots, tarragon, ½ teaspoon salt, and ¼ teaspoon pepper in small bowl and blend with fork.
3. Cut butter into 8 equal pieces.
4. Rinse drumsticks under cold running water and dry with paper towels. Cut a 2-inch-long by ½-inch-deep slit down the flat side of each drumstick, parallel to the bone. Using tip of paring knife, pry slit apart to make small pocket. Stuff each pocket with some of herb mixture, then push in piece of butter. Rinse and dry bowl.
5. Heat oil in large heavy-gauge skillet or sauté pan until very hot but not smoking. Add drumsticks to skillet,

pocket-sides-up, and fry over high heat, turning once or twice, about 10 minutes, or until golden brown.

6. Add wine and cover pan. Reduce heat to low and simmer 20 to 25 minutes, or until chicken is tender and juices run clear when drumsticks are pierced with tip of knife.

7. Using tongs, transfer drumsticks, pocket-sides-down, to heatproof serving platter, cover loosely with foil, and keep warm in 200-degree oven until ready to serve.

8. Raise heat under skillet to medium-high and reduce pan juices 3 to 4 minutes, or until thick enough to coat the back of a spoon.

9. Meanwhile, separate egg, placing yolk in small bowl and reserving white for another use.

10. Add cream to yolk and whisk until blended.

11. Whisking continuously, slowly add about ¼ cup of the reduced pan juices to cream mixture and whisk until well blended. Reduce heat under skillet to medium-low and, whisking continuously, gradually add sauce to pan. Simmer sauce 1 to 2 minutes, or until thickened. Do *not* allow sauce to boil.

12. Whisk in remaining ½ teaspoon salt and ¼ teaspoon pepper; taste and adjust seasoning. Pour ½ cup sauce over drumsticks and sprinkle with chopped parsley. Serve remaining sauce separately.

Sautéed Broccoli with Bacon and Onion

1 bunch broccoli (about 1¼ pounds)
Medium-size yellow onion
¼ pound sliced bacon
½ cup chicken stock
½ teaspoon salt
¼ teaspoon freshly ground black pepper

1. Wash and dry broccoli. Cut tops into florets. Trim stem ends, peel stems, if desired, and cut stems crosswise on diagonal into 1-inch pieces; set aside.

2. Halve, peel, and mince enough onion to measure 1 cup; set aside.

3. Coarsely chop bacon.

4. In medium-size heavy-gauge skillet or sauté pan, cook bacon over medium heat, stirring constantly, 2 to 3 minutes.

5. Add onion and sauté, stirring constantly, 2 to 3 minutes, or until onion is soft and transparent and bacon is cooked.

6. Add broccoli and cook over high heat, tossing gently, 1 minute.

7. Stir in chicken stock, salt, and pepper. Partially cover pan, reduce heat to medium, and cook 3 to 5 minutes, or until broccoli is tender.

8. Transfer broccoli to heatproof platter, cover with foil, and keep warm in 200-degree oven until ready to serve.

Glazed Carrots

4 large carrots (about 1 pound total weight), or 1 pound
   baby carrots
1 lemon

2 tablespoons unsalted butter
1 tablespoon honey
1 teaspoon salt
¼ teaspoon freshly ground black pepper
1 tablespoon chopped fresh parsley

1. Peel and trim carrots. If using large carrots, cut crosswise into thirds, then quarter each piece lengthwise; set carrots aside.

2. Squeeze enough lemon juice to measure 2 tablespoons; reserve remaining lemon for another use.

3. Combine carrots, lemon juice, butter, honey, ½ cup water, salt, and pepper in medium-size saucepan and bring to a boil over medium-high heat. Partially cover pan, reduce heat to medium-low, and cook gently 10 to 12 minutes, or until carrots are tender and sauce has reduced to a thick glaze.

4. Preheat oven to 200 degrees.

5. Turn carrots and glaze onto heatproof serving platter, cover loosely with foil, and keep warm in oven until ready to serve.

6. Just before serving, sprinkle carrots with parsley.

────────────

ADDED TOUCH

Unlike more delicate custards, this sturdy version does not curdle easily. Take care not to overcook it, though, or its surface will dimple.

Coconut Custard

1 cup half-and-half
½ cup heavy cream
3 large eggs
½ cup granulated sugar
⅓ cup sweetened flaked coconut
1 teaspoon vanilla extract
2 teaspoons cinnamon

1. Preheat oven to 325 degrees.

2. Combine half-and-half and cream in small nonaluminum saucepan and heat mixture over medium-low heat about 3 minutes until just scalded.

3. Meanwhile, separate 2 eggs, placing yolks in medium-size nonaluminum bowl and reserving whites for another use.

4. Add remaining whole egg and sugar to yolks, and whisk until well blended.

5. Whisking continuously, slowly add scalded cream mixture to egg mixture and whisk until blended. Stir in coconut and vanilla extract.

6. Divide mixture among 4 custard cups or 8-ounce ramekins and sprinkle each portion with ½ teaspoon cinnamon.

7. Place ramekins in 13 x 9 x 2-inch baking dish. Fill dish to a depth of 1 inch with warm water and bake custards, uncovered, 35 to 45 minutes, or until a knife inserted in the center comes out clean.

8. Remove custards from baking dish and set aside to cool slightly. Serve warm.

Roasted Game Hens Oriental-Style
Stir-Fried Snow Peas with Almonds
Sweet Red Pepper and Bean Sprout Salad

Cornish game hens, roasted until crispy, are accompanied by stir-fried snow peas with almonds and a sprout and red pepper salad.

The game hens are marinated in and basted with a robust sauce containing Chinese *hoisin* sauce, a sweet soybean-based mixture flavored with vinegar and spices. Look for *hoisin* sauce in cans or jars at Chinese groceries or in the Oriental foods section of well-stocked supermarkets.

SHOPPING LIST AND STAPLES

2 whole 1¼- to 1½-pound Rock Cornish game hens
2 medium-size red bell peppers, plus 1 small red bell pepper (optional)
½ pound snow peas
½ pound bean sprouts
2 cloves garlic
Small bunch Italian parsley (optional)
2 tablespoons chicken stock, preferably homemade (see page 12), or canned
2 tablespoons Oriental sesame oil, approximately
1½ tablespoons Chinese rice vinegar
¼ cup hoisin sauce, if available
¼ cup Chinese soy sauce, plus 1 tablespoon if not using hoisin sauce
1½ tablespoons ketchup, or 3 tablespoons if not using hoisin sauce
3½-ounce can sliced almonds

1 tablespoon light brown sugar
2 teaspoons granulated sugar
Salt

UTENSILS

Large heavy-gauge skillet
Small roasting pan
Small saucepan
Medium-size bowl
3 small bowls
Colander
Measuring cups and spoons
Chef's knife
Paring knife
2 wooden spoons
Bulb baster or basting brush
Poultry shears

START-TO-FINISH STEPS

1. Follow game hens recipe steps 1 through 5.
2. While hens are marinating, follow salad recipe steps 1 through 3.
3. Follow game hens recipe step 6.
4. While hens are roasting, follow salad recipe steps 4 and 5, and snow peas recipe steps 1 and 2.
5. Follow game hens recipe steps 7 through 9.
6. Follow snow peas recipe steps 3 through 6, and game hens recipe step 10, and serve with salad.

RECIPES

Roasted Game Hens Oriental-Style

2 whole 1¼- to 1½-pound Rock Cornish game hens

Marinade:
2 cloves garlic
¼ cup hoisin sauce, if available
2 tablespoons Chinese soy sauce, or 3 tablespoons if not using hoisin sauce
1½ tablespoons ketchup, or 3 tablespoons if not using hoisin sauce
1 tablespoon light brown sugar
1 teaspoon Oriental sesame oil, or 1½ teaspoons if not using hoisin sauce

Garnishes (optional):
8 sprigs Italian parsley
Small red bell pepper

1. Rinse game hens and dry with paper towels. Remove and discard any excess fat or cartilage from cavity and neck. Place game hens in roasting pan; set aside.
2. Bruise garlic cloves under flat blade of chef's knife; remove peel and discard. Mince garlic and place in small bowl.
3. Add hoisin sauce, if using, soy sauce, ketchup, sugar, and sesame oil, and stir until blended.
4. Pour sauce over hens, completely coating outside and cavity of each hen; set aside to marinate at least 10 minutes.
5. Preheat oven to 375 degrees.
6. Turn hens breast-side-down and roast 25 minutes, basting occasionally.
7. Turn hens breast-side-up and roast another 20 minutes, basting occasionally.
8. Meanwhile, wash parsley, if using, and pat dry with paper towels. Trim stems and discard. Set aside.
9. Wash red bell pepper, if using, and dry with paper towel. Halve, core, and seed pepper. Cut one half lengthwise into ¼-inch-wide strips; reserve remainder for another use.
10. Remove hens from oven and split in half with poultry shears. Transfer to 4 dinner plates and garnish each serving with parsley sprigs and bell pepper strips, if desired.

Stir-Fried Snow Peas with Almonds

½ pound snow peas
2 tablespoons chicken stock
1 teaspoon salt
½ teaspoon granulated sugar
1½ teaspoons Oriental sesame oil
1 cup sliced almonds

1. Trim ends and remove strings from snow peas. Place snow peas in colander, rinse under cold running water, and set aside to drain.
2. Combine chicken stock, salt, and sugar in small bowl, and stir until sugar dissolves; set aside.
3. Place large heavy-gauge skillet over medium-high heat. Add sesame oil and heat, swirling oil to coat pan, about 45 seconds, or until oil is just about to smoke. Add snow

peas and stir fry about 1 minute, or until vivid green in color.

4. Add stock mixture to skillet and cook snow peas, tossing gently, 1 minute.

5. Add sliced almonds and toss until almonds are evenly distributed and coated with sauce.

6. Divide snow peas and almonds among dinner plates and serve immediately.

Sweet Red Pepper and Bean Sprout Salad

2 medium-size red bell peppers
½ pound bean sprouts
2 tablespoons Chinese soy sauce
1½ tablespoons Chinese rice vinegar
1½ teaspoons Oriental sesame oil
1½ teaspoons granulated sugar
1 teaspoon salt

1. Bring 1 quart water to a boil in small saucepan over high heat.

2. Meanwhile, halve, core, and seed red bell peppers. Cut peppers lengthwise into ⅛-inch-wide strips. You should have about 1 cup strips. Plunge pepper strips into boiling water and cook about 15 seconds. Turn into colander and immediately refresh under cold running water. Drain thoroughly and dry with paper towels. Place red pepper strips in medium-size bowl; set aside.

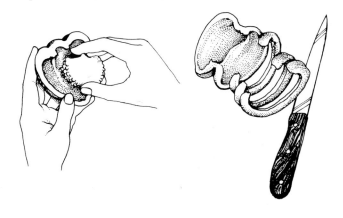

3. Place bean sprouts in colander and rinse gently under cold running water. Drain thoroughly and dry with paper towels. Add to bowl with pepper strips.

4. For dressing, combine soy sauce, rice vinegar, sesame oil, sugar, and salt in small bowl and stir until sugar dissolves.

5. Pour dressing over bean sprouts and peppers, and toss gently until evenly coated. Cover with plastic wrap and set aside until ready to serve.

ADDED TOUCH

These poached pears are infused with the delicate tang of fresh ginger. Serve them with sugar cookies.

Poached Pears with Vanilla Ice Cream

1 cup granulated sugar
2 cinnamon sticks
Six ⅛-inch-thick slices fresh ginger (about ½ ounce)
1 lemon
4 slightly underripe medium-size Anjou or Bosc pears
3 slices candied ginger
1 pint vanilla ice cream

1. Combine sugar, 2 cups water, cinnamon sticks, and ginger in medium-size sauté pan and bring to a boil over medium-high heat, stirring constantly to dissolve sugar. Cook about 5 to 7 minutes, or until sugar has dissolved completely.

2. Meanwhile, wash lemon and dry with paper towel. Using sharp paring knife or zester, cut four 1-inch-long strips of rind; set aside. Halve lemon and squeeze juice from both halves.

3. Using vegetable peeler or sharp paring knife, peel pears. Halve each pear lengthwise; remove and discard cores. Place pear halves on large plate and sprinkle with lemon juice to prevent discoloration.

4. Add pear halves to syrup and return liquid to a boil. Reduce heat to low and poach pears, turning occasionally, about 15 minutes, or until tender when pierced with tip of knife.

5. Meanwhile, cut candied ginger and lemon rind into fine julienne strips.

6. Using slotted spoon, transfer poached pear halves to 4 dessert bowls and set aside.

7. Remove cinnamon sticks and ginger from poaching liquid. Add candied ginger and lemon rind, raise heat to high, and reduce liquid for about 15 to 20 minutes, or until thick and syrupy.

8. Spoon syrup over pears, cover with plastic wrap, and refrigerate at least 2 hours, or until chilled.

9. Just before serving, top each serving with a scoop of vanilla ice cream.

Marianne Langan

M arianne Langan loves to prepare meals for her family. "I became a creative cook," she says, "to make eating fun for them." Their favorite meal? Fried chicken. In Menu 1, she coats chicken pieces with a beer-based batter and then pan fries them until they are crisp and golden—a variation on the standard deep-fry recipe, which, in fact, originated in Austria, not in the American South. Other fixings for this homey meal include an herbed potato salad and cornmeal muffins.

Menu 2, another Langan family favorite, also has foreign roots. This Italian meal begins with a bountiful antipasto platter of vegetables and salami to which everyone helps themselves. The antipasto is followed by chicken and vegetables in tomato sauce on a bed of *capellini* pasta, and a tossed salad with Parmesan cheese dressing.

Menu 3 is decidedly American. The Buffalo chicken legs are the cook's adaptation of a chicken-wing recipe that originated in Buffalo, New York, in the mid-1960s. The deep-fried drumsticks are brushed with hot sauce and accompanied by a bowl of blue cheese sauce with crudités to cool the palate. A filling casserole of baked ham, cheese, tomato, and bread, an American classic, can be served with or after the chicken legs.

For a hearty dinner, serve crisp batter-dipped chicken pieces with potato salad and buttered cornmeal muffins. Glasses of iced tea go well with this meal.

65

Crispy Fried Chicken
New Potato Salad
Bacon-Corn Muffins

A simple beer batter provides the flavorful coating for the pan-fried chicken. For the best results when frying chicken, select a skillet wide enough to hold all the pieces comfortably without overlapping. If the pan is crowded, the moisture from the chicken will not evaporate, and it will stew rather than brown. If necessary, fry the chicken pieces in several batches.

Select new red potatoes for the salad: They are best for boiling because they are low in starch and hold their shape well. The skins are so thin and tender that the potatoes do not need paring. For an interesting variation, omit the celery seeds and add 2 tablespoons of fresh snipped dill instead.

SHOPPING LIST AND STAPLES

3½-pound frying chicken, cut into pieces, or 3½ pounds chicken parts
4 slices bacon (3 to 4 ounces)
1½ pounds small new red potatoes
Small bunch celery
Small bunch scallions
Small bunch parsley
Small clove garlic
1 lemon (optional)
3 eggs
1 cup milk
1 stick unsalted butter (optional)
4 cups vegetable oil
¾ cup mayonnaise
2 tablespoons red wine vinegar
1½ teaspoons prepared mustard
1⅔ cups all-purpose flour
1 cup yellow cornmeal
2 tablespoons granulated sugar
1 tablespoon plus ¼ teaspoon baking powder
¼ teaspoon celery seeds
¼ teaspoon paprika
Salt
Freshly ground pepper
7-ounce bottle beer

UTENSILS

Very large, deep heavy-gauge skillet
Medium-size skillet
Large saucepan with cover
Small saucepan with cover
12-cup muffin pan
Colander
3 large bowls
3 small bowls
Measuring cups and spoons
Chef's knife
Wooden spoon
Rubber spatula
Wire whisk
Metal tongs
Vegetable brush
Deep-fat thermometer (optional)

START-TO-FINISH STEPS

One hour ahead: Bring 3 eggs to room temperature.

1. Wash parsley and pat dry with paper towels. Trim ends and discard. Set aside 4 sprigs, if using for garnish for chicken recipe; chop enough parsley to measure 2 tablespoons for potato salad recipe; reserve remainder for another use.
2. Follow potato salad recipe steps 1 through 6.
3. Follow chicken recipe steps 1 through 7.
4. While chicken is frying, follow potato salad recipe steps 7 through 10 and muffins recipe steps 1 and 2.
5. Turn chicken if you haven't already, and follow muffins recipe steps 3 through 9.
6. While muffins are baking, follow chicken recipe steps 8 and 9.
7. Follow potato salad recipe steps 11 and 12.
8. Follow chicken recipe step 10 and muffins recipe step 10.
9. Follow chicken recipe step 11 and serve with potato salad and muffins.

RECIPES

Crispy Fried Chicken

Small clove garlic
⅔ cup unsifted all-purpose flour
¼ teaspoon baking powder
½ teaspoon salt
¼ teaspoon paprika
⅓ cup beer
1 egg, at room temperature
4 cups vegetable oil

3½-pound frying chicken, cut into pieces, or 3½ pounds chicken parts
1 lemon for garnish (optional)
4 parsley sprigs for garnish (optional)

1. Peel and mince garlic.
2. Combine garlic, flour, baking powder, salt, and paprika in large bowl and stir with fork to combine.
3. Combine beer, egg, and 1 tablespoon oil in small bowl and beat lightly with fork until well blended. Add beer mixture to dry ingredients and stir with fork until blended.
4. Heat remaining oil in very large, deep heavy-gauge skillet over medium-high heat until deep-fat thermometer registers 375 degrees, or until a small cube of bread dropped in oil rises to the surface surrounded by bubbles.
5. Meanwhile, wash chicken under cold running water and dry thoroughly with paper towels; set aside.
6. Dip chicken in beer batter, several pieces at a time, and turn to coat evenly. Using tongs, transfer chicken pieces to skillet, allowing excess batter to drip off before carefully lowering chicken into hot oil. Fry 2 minutes on each side.
7. Turn chicken and fry 30 minutes, turning after 15 minutes.
8. If using lemon, wash and dry with paper towel. Cut four ¼-inch-thick slices from center of lemon and set aside.
9. Line platter with double thickness of paper towels.
10. Using tongs, transfer chicken to paper-towel-lined platter to drain.
11. Divide chicken pieces among dinner plates and garnish each serving with 1 lemon slice and a parsley sprig, if desired.

New Potato Salad

1½ pounds small new red potatoes
1 teaspoon salt
1 egg, at room temperature
Small bunch scallions
2 stalks celery
2 tablespoons chopped parsley

Dressing:
¾ cup mayonnaise
2 tablespoons red wine vinegar
1½ teaspoons prepared mustard
¼ teaspoon celery seeds
½ teaspoon salt
Pinch of freshly ground pepper

1. Scrub potatoes under cold running water and rinse. Place potatoes in large saucepan, add salt, and enough cold water to cover, and bring to a boil over high heat. Reduce heat to medium and boil potatoes, partially covered, 10 minutes.
2. Place egg in small saucepan with enough cold water to cover and bring to a boil over medium-high heat. Cover pan, remove from heat, and set aside undisturbed 15 minutes.

3. Meanwhile, wash scallions and dry with paper towels; trim ends and discard. Cut enough scallions crosswise into ¼-inch pieces to measure ¾ cup; set aside. Reserve remaining scallions for another use.
4. Wash celery and dry with paper towel; trim ends and discard. Cut enough celery crosswise into ¼-inch pieces to measure ⅔ cup; set aside.
5. Turn potatoes into colander and set aside to cool.
6. Drain egg and refill pan with cold water; set aside to cool.
7. When egg is cool enough to handle, peel and discard shell. Place egg in small bowl, cover with plastic wrap, and refrigerate.
8. For dressing, combine mayonnaise, vinegar, mustard, celery seeds, salt, and pepper in small bowl, and beat with fork until well blended; set aside.
9. Dry potatoes with paper towels and cut crosswise into ¼-inch-thick slices.
10. In large bowl, combine potatoes, scallions, celery, and parsley, and toss gently to combine. Add dressing and toss until evenly coated. Cover with plastic wrap and refrigerate until ready to serve.
11. Cut egg crosswise into ⅛-inch-thick slices.
12. Divide potato salad among 4 dinner plates and top each serving with a few egg slices.

Bacon-Corn Muffins

4 slices bacon (3 to 4 ounces)
1 cup yellow cornmeal
1 cup all-purpose flour
2 tablespoons granulated sugar
1 tablespoon baking powder
¾ teaspoon salt
1 cup milk
1 egg, at room temperature
1 stick unsalted butter (optional)

1. Preheat oven to 425 degrees.
2. Line plate with double thickness of paper towels; set aside.
3. In medium-size skillet, cook bacon over medium-high heat, turning to cook evenly, 3 to 4 minutes, or until crisp.
4. With tongs, transfer bacon to paper-towel-lined plate to drain; reserve drippings in skillet. Crumble bacon; set aside.
5. Grease 12-cup muffin pan; set aside.
6. In large bowl, combine cornmeal, flour, sugar, baking powder, and salt, and stir with fork to combine; set aside.
7. In small bowl, combine milk, egg, and 3 tablespoons bacon drippings, and whisk until blended.
8. Add milk mixture to dry ingredients all at once. Add crumbled bacon and stir with fork just until moistened.
9. Spoon batter into prepared muffin pan, filling each cup two-thirds full, and bake 15 minutes, or until muffins are puffed and golden.
10. Turn muffins into napkin-lined basket and serve hot, with butter if desired.

Antipasto
Chicken and Vegetables in Tomato Sauce with Capellini
Tossed Salad with Parmesan Dressing

An antipasto (meaning literally "before the food") is a customary offering at Italian meals. Intended to whet the appetite, an antipasto platter may include a wide sampling of ingredients, as this recipe shows.

SHOPPING LIST AND STAPLES

2 whole boneless, skinless chicken breasts, halved (about 1½ pounds total weight)
2 to 4 ounces thinly sliced Italian salami

This colorful Italian dinner includes a meat and vegetable antipasto with watercress dressing, a main course of chicken, vegetables, and pasta, and a colorful tossed salad.

2 small heads salad greens, such as romaine, Boston, leaf lettuce, or chicory, in any combination
Small head red leaf lettuce
Small bunch watercress
¾ pound medium-size mushrooms
Small bunch red radishes
Medium-size zucchini (about ½ pound)
¼ pound fresh green beans
Small green, red, and yellow bell pepper
Small cucumber
6-ounce package alfalfa sprouts (½ cup)
Medium-size yellow onion
Small red onion
4 small cloves garlic
Small bunch fresh chives

Small bunch fresh basil, or ½ teaspoon dried
¾ cup chicken stock, preferably homemade
   (see page 12), or canned
28-ounce can Italian plum tomatoes
8-ounce jar fava beans
1 egg
2 ounces Parmesan cheese
10-ounce package frozen artichoke hearts
½ cup vegetable oil
½ cup plus 3 tablespoons olive oil
¼ cup plus 2 tablespoons balsamic or red wine vinegar
4¾-ounce jar pimiento-stuffed green olives
8 ounces dried capellini
¼ teaspoon dried oregano
Salt and freshly ground black and white pepper

UTENSILS

Food processor or blender
Large heavy-gauge skillet with cover
Large saucepan
Medium-size saucepan
2 serving platters, one heatproof
Salad bowl
Small bowl
Colander

Large strainer
Measuring cups and spoons
Chef's knife
Paring knife
Wooden spoon
Rubber spatula
Wire whisk
Vegetable brush
Grater (if not using processor)
Rolling pin

START-TO-FINISH STEPS

One hour ahead: Set out artichokes to thaw for antipasto recipe.

1. Prepare all greens, herbs, and garlic for all recipes.
2. Follow antipasto recipe steps 1 through 8.
3. Follow salad recipe steps 1 through 6.
4. Follow chicken recipe steps 1 through 7.
5. Follow salad recipe steps 7 and 8.
6. Follow chicken recipe step 8 and salad recipe step 9.
7. Follow chicken recipe steps 9 and 10.
8. Follow antipasto recipe step 9 and serve as first course.
9. Follow chicken recipe steps 11 and 12.
10. Follow salad recipe step 10, chicken recipe step 13, and serve.

Antipasto

Salt
¼ pound fresh green beans
8-ounce jar fava beans
Small red bell pepper
Small cucumber
10-ounce package frozen artichoke hearts, thawed
¼ cup pimiento-stuffed green olives
8 leaves red leaf lettuce
2 to 4 ounces thinly sliced Italian salami

Dressing:
½ cup olive oil
2 tablespoons balsamic or red wine vinegar
½ cup firmly packed watercress leaves
Small clove garlic, crushed and peeled
Freshly ground pepper

1. Bring 1 quart lightly salted water to a boil in medium-size saucepan over high heat.
2. While water is heating, trim ends of green beans. Plunge beans into boiling water and cook 3 minutes.
3. Rinse fava beans in strainer; set aside to drain.
4. Refresh green beans in colander under cold water; drain.
5. Wash and dry red pepper. Halve, core, and seed pepper. Quarter each half lengthwise; set aside.
6. Wash and dry cucumber. Halve crosswise. Using fork, score one half lengthwise and then cut crosswise into ¼-inch-thick slices. Reserve remaining half for another use.
7. Pat artichoke hearts dry with paper towels. Drain olives.
8. Line serving platter with lettuce; arrange vegetables, olives, and salami attractively on lettuce. Cover with plastic wrap and refrigerate until ready to serve.
9. In food processor or blender process dressing ingredients until smooth. Add salt and pepper to taste. Turn dressing into small pitcher and serve with antipasto.

Chicken and Vegetables in Tomato Sauce with Capellini

Medium-size zucchini (about ½ pound)
8 medium-size mushrooms (about 6 ounces)
Medium-size yellow onion
28-ounce can Italian plum tomatoes
2 whole boneless, skinless chicken breasts, halved
3 tablespoons olive oil
¾ cup chicken stock
2 teaspoons minced garlic
1 tablespoon chopped fresh basil, or ½ teaspoon dried
Salt and freshly ground white pepper
8 ounces dried capellini

1. Scrub, rinse, and dry zucchini. Cut enough crosswise into ¼-inch slices to measure 1 cup.
2. Wipe mushrooms clean with damp paper towels. Trim stems and discard. Cut enough mushrooms into ¼-inch-thick slices to measure 1½ cups; set aside.
3. Coarsely chop enough onion to measure 1 cup.
4. Drain tomatoes, reserving juice for another use. Chop enough tomatoes to measure 2½ cups and set aside.
5. Preheat oven to 200 degrees.
6. Wash chicken breasts and pat dry with paper towels. Cut into 3-inch-long by ½-inch-wide strips; set aside.
7. In large heavy-gauge skillet, heat 2 tablespoons oil over medium-high heat. Add chicken and sauté, stirring occasionally, 4 minutes, or until browned.
8. Add zucchini, mushrooms, and onion, and sauté 2 to 3 minutes, or until vegetables are slightly softened.
9. Add tomatoes, stock, minced garlic, basil, 1 teaspoon salt, and pepper to skillet, and stir to combine. Reduce heat to medium-low, cover skillet, and simmer 15 minutes, or until chicken and vegetables are fork-tender.
10. Bring 3 quarts water, 1 tablespoon oil, and 1 tablespoon salt to a boil in large saucepan over medium heat.
11. Place heatproof serving platter in oven to warm.
12. Add pasta to boiling water; stir to separate strands. Cook 8 to 10 minutes, or just until *al dente.* Drain.
13. Transfer pasta to warm serving platter, top with chicken and vegetables, and serve.

Tossed Salad with Parmesan Dressing

6 red radishes
Small yellow and green bell pepper
½ cup alfalfa sprouts
8 medium-size mushrooms (about 6 ounces)
Small red onion
4 cups mixed salad greens such as romaine, Boston, leaf lettuce, or chicory, in any combination

Dressing:
2 ounces Parmesan cheese
¼ teaspoon dried oregano
½ cup vegetable oil
¼ cup balsamic or red wine vinegar
1 egg
Small clove garlic, crushed and peeled
2 tablespoons minced fresh chives
½ teaspoon salt

1. Wash, dry, and trim radishes. Cut into thin slices.
2. Wash and dry bell peppers. Halve, core, and seed peppers. Cut lengthwise into ¼-inch-wide strips; set aside.
3. Rinse and dry sprouts; set aside.
4. Clean mushrooms with damp paper towels. Trim stems and discard. Cut mushrooms into ¼-inch slices.
5. Peel onion and slice thinly; separate into rings.
6. Place greens in salad bowl and top with vegetables. Cover and refrigerate until ready to serve.
7. Grate enough Parmesan to measure ¼ cup.
8. With rolling pin, crush oregano between 2 sheets of waxed paper.
9. Combine cheese, oregano, and remaining dressing ingredients in food processor or blender and process until smooth. Transfer to small bowl, cover, and set aside.
10. When ready to serve, whisk dressing briefly to recombine and pour over salad. Toss until evenly coated.

Buffalo Chicken Legs with Blue Cheese Sauce
Baked Ham, Cheese, and Tomato Casserole
Vegetable Sauté with Mandarin Oranges

Spicy chicken legs with sautéed vegetables and orange slices and a ham, cheese, and tomato casserole make satisfying family fare.

The tomato, ham, and cheese bake is also known as a strata, or layered casserole. Stratas were probably originally devised as a way to use up stale bread. This dish is ideal for busy cooks because it tastes best when assembled several hours in advance, or even the night before, and refrigerated.

SHOPPING LIST AND STAPLES

8 small chicken legs (about 1½ pounds total weight)
⅓ pound baked ham, thinly sliced
2 large carrots (about ½ pound total weight)

Medium-size zucchini (about ½ pound)
Small bunch celery
1 large or 3 small ripe tomatoes
Small yellow onion
Small bunch scallions
Small bunch parsley
Small clove garlic
10-ounce can mandarin orange segments
3 eggs
3 cups plus 2 tablespoons milk
1 stick unsalted butter or margarine
½ pound Jarlsberg or Swiss cheese, thinly sliced

71

1 ounce blue cheese
8-ounce container plain low-fat yogurt
4 cups vegetable oil
⅓ cup hot pepper sauce (optional)
12-inch loaf French or Italian bread, or
    two 6-inch hero rolls
1 teaspoon dry mustard
¼ teaspoon dried tarragon
Salt and freshly ground pepper

UTENSILS

Large heavy-gauge saucepan or deep fryer
Medium-size sauté pan with cover
Steamer unit, or saucepan large enough to accommodate
    collapsible vegetable steamer, with cover
8 x 8-inch baking dish
Collapsible vegetable steamer (if not using steamer unit)
Medium-size bowl
2 small bowls
Measuring cups and spoons
Chef's knife
Paring knife
Serrated bread knife
Wooden spoon
Rubber spatula
Wire whisk
Metal tongs
Vegetable peeler
Vegetable brush
Basting brush
Deep-fat thermometer (optional)
Mortar and pestle (optional)
Rolling pin (if not using mortar and pestle)

START-TO-FINISH STEPS

1. Halve, peel, and mince enough onion to measure 2 tablespoons for casserole recipe.
2. Follow casserole recipe steps 1 through 10.
3. While casserole is baking, follow vegetables recipe steps 1 through 6.
4. Follow chicken recipe steps 1 through 7.
5. While chicken is frying, follow vegetables recipe steps 7 through 10.
6. Follow chicken recipe steps 8 through 10, vegetables recipe step 11, and serve with casserole.

RECIPES

Buffalo Chicken Legs with Blue Cheese Sauce

Small bunch scallions
2 stalks celery with leafy tops
4 cups vegetable oil
½ cup plain low-fat yogurt
2 tablespoons milk
¼ cup crumbled blue cheese

8 small chicken legs (about 1½ pounds total weight)
⅓ cup hot pepper sauce (optional)

1. Wash scallions and dry with paper towels. Trim ends and discard. Halve 4 scallions lengthwise; reserve remainder for another use.
2. Wash celery and dry with paper towels; do not trim leafy tops. Halve stalks lengthwise, then cut crosswise into 3- to 4-inch pieces; set aside.
3. In large heavy-gauge saucepan or deep fryer, heat oil until deep-fat thermometer registers 375 degrees, or until a cube of bread dropped in oil rises to the top surrounded by bubbles.
4. Combine yogurt, milk, and cheese in small bowl and stir until well blended; the sauce will remain somewhat lumpy. Divide among 4 small serving bowls; set aside.
5. Wash chicken and dry thoroughly with paper towels.
6. Line platter with double thickness of paper towels.
7. With tongs, carefully lower chicken legs into hot oil and fry 7 to 8 minutes, or until browned and juices run clear when chicken is pierced with tip of knife.
8. Transfer chicken to towel-lined platter to drain.
9. Brush hot pepper sauce evenly over legs, if desired.
10. Divide chicken legs, celery, and scallions among 4 dinner plates, and serve with sauce on the side.

Baked Ham, Cheese, and Tomato Casserole

1 large or 3 small ripe tomatoes
6 thin slices Jarlsberg or Swiss cheese
6 thin slices baked ham
Small clove garlic
4 tablespoons unsalted butter or margarine, at room
    temperature
1 teaspoon dry mustard
12-inch loaf French or Italian bread, or two 6-inch
    hero rolls
3 cups milk
3 eggs
2 tablespoons minced onion
Salt and freshly ground pepper

1. Preheat oven to 375 degrees.
2. Butter 8 x 8-inch baking dish; set aside.
3. Wash tomato(es) and dry with paper towel. Core and cut into total of 12 slices; set aside.
4. Halve cheese and ham slices; set aside.
5. Peel and mince garlic; set aside.
6. Combine butter, garlic, and ½ teaspoon dry mustard in small bowl and stir until well blended; set aside.
7. Cut bread into 1-inch-thick slices. Spread one side of each slice with butter mixture.
8. Top buttered side of each bread slice with 1 slice each of tomato, ham, and cheese, folding ham and cheese to fit bread, and place in prepared dish, standing in 3 rows of 4 slices each.
9. In medium-size bowl, combine milk, eggs, onion, remaining dry mustard, 1 teaspoon salt, and a pinch of pepper, and whisk until blended.

10. Pour milk mixture evenly over casserole and bake 45 minutes, or until puffed and golden.

Vegetable Sauté with Mandarin Oranges

2 large carrots (about ½ pound total weight)
Medium-size zucchini (about ½ pound)
2 stalks celery
Small bunch parsley
¼ teaspoon dried tarragon
½ cup canned mandarin orange segments
1 teaspoon salt
3 tablespoons unsalted butter

1. Peel and trim carrots. Halve each carrot lengthwise, then cut each half crosswise into 3-inch pieces. Cut each piece lengthwise into ¼-inch julienne; set aside.
2. Scrub zucchini under cold running water; rinse, and dry with paper towel. Trim ends and discard. Halve zucchini lengthwise, then cut each half crosswise into 3-inch pieces. Cut lengthwise into ¼-inch julienne; set aside.
3. Wash celery and dry with paper towels. Trim stem ends and leafy tops, and discard. Cut each stalk crosswise into 3-inch pieces, then cut each piece lengthwise into ¼-inch julienne; set aside.
4. Wash parsley and dry with paper towels. Trim stem ends and discard. Chop enough parsley to measure ¼ cup; reserve remainder for another use.
5. Crush tarragon in mortar with pestle or place between 2 sheets of waxed paper and crush with rolling pin; set aside.
6. Drain oranges; set aside.
7. In bottom of steamer unit or saucepan large enough to accommodate collapsible steamer, bring 2 cups of water to a boil over medium-high heat.
8. Place vegetables in steamer. Sprinkle vegetables with salt and tarragon, cover pan, and steam 4 minutes, or to desired doneness.
9. Meanwhile, melt butter in medium-size sauté pan over medium-low heat.
10. Add steamed vegetables to butter and toss until evenly coated. Cover pan and keep warm until ready to serve.
11. Add mandarin oranges and toss briefly. Divide vegetables and oranges among dinner plates. Sprinkle each serving with 1 tablespoon parsley, and serve.

ADDED TOUCH

A glass of cold milk is the ideal partner for this moist orange chocolate cake, which takes about an hour to make including baking and frosting.

Orange Chocolate Cake

¾ cup Dutch-process unsweetened cocoa powder, approximately
3 eggs
1 stick plus 4 tablespoons unsalted butter or margarine, at room temperature

1½ cups granulated sugar
2 tablespoons freshly squeezed orange juice
1 tablespoon grated orange zest
1 teaspoon vanilla extract
2¼ cups unsifted all-purpose flour
1 tablespoon baking powder
1 teaspoon baking soda
¼ teaspoon salt
1 cup milk
1 orange for garnish (optional)
Creamy Orange Frosting (see following recipe)

1. Preheat oven to 350 degrees.
2. Butter two 8-inch round cake pans. Add 1 tablespoon cocoa powder to each pan and tilt and rotate pans to coat evenly; set aside.
3. Separate eggs, dropping whites into medium-size bowl and placing yolks in small bowl; set aside.
4. In large mixing bowl, cream butter with sugar until light and fluffy.
5. Add egg yolks, one at a time, beating after each addition until totally incorporated.
6. Beat in orange juice, orange zest, and vanilla; set aside.
7. Combine flour, ½ cup cocoa, baking powder, baking soda, and salt in another large bowl, and stir to blend.
8. In thirds, alternately add dry ingredients and milk to batter, beating well after each addition and scraping down sides of bowl occasionally; set aside.
9. Beat egg whites with electric mixer at high speed until soft peaks form. Using rubber spatula, gently fold whites into batter.
10. Divide batter evenly between prepared pans and bake 35 minutes, or until toothpick inserted in center of each layer comes out clean.
11. Transfer pans to wire racks and set aside to cool 10 minutes.
12. Invert pans over racks and turn out cake layers; cool completely before frosting.
13. Peel orange, if using, removing as much white pith as possible. With sharp paring knife, segment orange.
14. Frost cake with creamy orange frosting and garnish with orange segments, if desired.

Creamy Orange Frosting

4 tablespoons unsalted butter or margarine, at room temperature
3-ounce package cream cheese, at room temperature
2 to 4 tablespoons freshly squeezed orange juice
1 tablespoon grated orange zest
4 to 5 cups confectioners' sugar

1. Combine butter and cream cheese in large bowl and beat with electric mixer until light and fluffy.
2. Beat in 2 tablespoons orange juice and orange zest.
3. Gradually add 4 cups sugar, beating at medium speed and scraping down sides of bowl occasionally, until frosting is of good spreading consistency. If necessary, add more orange juice and/or sugar.

Loni Kuhn

MENU 1 (Right)
Nachos
Mazatlán Sopa Seca
Tossed Salad

MENU 2
Guacamole Salad
Chicken Burritos with
Mexican Rice and Salsa Cruda

MENU 3
Tortilla Soup
Beef Tacos with Green Salsa
Confetti Vegetables

Having traveled extensively through Mexico, Loni Kuhn admits to a passion for the lively foods of that country. "I am fascinated by the history of the native cuisine," she says, "because it is a marvelous amalgam of European and indigenous ingredients." The menus she offers here are adaptations of complicated Mexican recipes tailored to American tastes and kitchens.

The Pacific coast resort of Mazatlán is one of her favorite Mexican cities, and its foods are the inspiration for Menu 1. *Nachos,* snacks made with tortilla chips and a selection of toppings, start the meal and are followed by a *sopa seca,* or "dry soup," which always contains rice, pasta, or tortillas but is not really a soup at all. In Mexico, it usually follows a wet soup and is served before the main course. Loni Kuhn's version *is* the entrée and combines vermicelli and shrimp (Mazatlán is a shrimping port) with onions, tomatoes, and green chilies.

Northern Mexico's cooking is the focus of Menu 2. The guacamole salad is flavored with piquant *tomatillos* (tiny green tomato-like fruits), and the accompanying *burritos* consist of soft wheat-flour tortillas enclosing chicken, chilies, and cheese. For extra bite, spoon *salsa cruda* (uncooked tomato-chili sauce) over the *burritos* before rolling them. The Mexican rice can be served in the *burritos* or as a side dish.

In Menu 3, the cook features corn tortillas, the flat bread eaten in central and southern Mexico. A light, elegant tortilla soup containing shredded Monterey Jack cheese and sliced avocados is served with beef tacos— folded corn tortillas with a hearty beef filling.

Start off this buffet dinner with an appetizer platter of assemble-your-own nachos—tortilla chips, cheese, chilies, jícama, and coriander. Then bring on the shrimp and pasta "soup" and a romaine salad tossed with a mustard vinaigrette.

Nachos
Mazatlán Sopa Seca
Tossed Salad

For this unbroiled version of *nachos,* guests pile a variety of ingredients, including jícama, on tortilla chips. Jícama is a crunchy tuber that looks like a turnip and tastes like a cross between an apple and a water chestnut. You can buy it whole or cut up in well-stocked supermarkets and in Mexican groceries. Store whole jícama in a plastic bag in the refrigerator; cut-up jícama will keep for up to two weeks immersed in water in a covered container if refrigerated.

To save time, you can make the tortilla chips well ahead of serving and freeze them. They will keep for up to six months.

SHOPPING LIST AND STAPLES

1 pound medium-size shrimp
1 pound jícama
4 fresh jalapeño or mild green Anaheim chilies, or
    4-ounce can whole chilies
Medium-size red bell pepper
2 medium-size tomatoes
Small head romaine lettuce
Medium-size onion
2 cloves garlic
Small bunch coriander
Large lemon
½ pound Monterey Jack cheese
8-ounce container sour cream (optional)
4 fresh corn tortillas, or 11-ounce bag tortilla chips
2 cups chicken stock, preferably homemade (see page 12),
    or canned
5¾-ounce can pitted black olives
4-ounce can diced mild green Anaheim chilies
10-ounce package frozen corn kernels
4 cups plus 3 tablespoons vegetable oil
    (if using fresh tortillas)
⅓ cup olive oil
2 teaspoons prepared mustard
8 ounces vermicelli
Salt
Freshly ground pepper

UTENSILS

Large heavy-gauge skillet with cover
Medium-size heavy-gauge skillet (if using fresh tortillas)
Salad bowl
Small nonaluminum bowl
Salad spinner (optional)
Colander
Strainer
Measuring cups and spoons
Cleaver (optional)
Chef's knife
Paring knife
2 wooden spoons
Mesh strainer or slotted spatula (if using fresh tortillas)
Whisk
Metal tongs
Vegetable peeler (optional)
Deep-fat thermometer (if using fresh tortillas)
Rubber gloves (if using fresh chilies)

START-TO-FINISH STEPS

One hour ahead: Cut package of frozen corn kernels in half with cleaver or sharp chef's knife. Place one half in freezer bag and return to freezer for another use. Set out remaining half to thaw for salad recipe.

1. Wash coriander and pat dry with paper towels. Trim stem ends and discard. Measure 1 cup loosely packed sprigs, if using, for nachos recipe, and chop enough remaining coriander to measure 1 tablespoon for sopa seca recipe; set aside. Under flat blade of chef's knife, crush garlic for sopa seca and salad recipes. Remove peels and discard. Set garlic aside.
2. Follow salad recipe steps 1 through 6.
3. Follow nachos recipe steps 1 through 9.
4. Follow sopa seca recipe steps 1 through 9.
5. While sopa seca simmers, serve nachos as first course.
6. Follow sopa seca recipe steps 10 through 12, salad recipe step 7, and serve.

RECIPES

Nachos

½ pound Monterey Jack cheese
1 pound jícama
4 fresh jalapeño or mild green Anaheim chilies,
    or 4-ounce can whole chilies
4 cups vegetable oil (if using fresh tortillas)
4 fresh corn tortillas, or 11-ounce bag tortilla chips
1 cup loosely packed coriander sprigs (optional)

1. Cut cheese into ⅛- to ¼-inch-thick slices; set aside.
2. Peel jícama and cut into ⅛-inch-thick slices; set aside.
3. Wearing rubber gloves, rinse fresh chilies, if using, and dry with paper towels. Trim stem ends and discard. Split each chili lengthwise; remove seeds and discard. Cut each chili lengthwise into ½-inch-wide strips; set aside. If using canned chilies, turn into strainer and rinse under cold running water. Drain chilies and dry with paper towels. Proceed as for fresh chilies.
4. If using fresh tortillas, heat oil in medium-size heavy-gauge skillet over medium-high heat until deep-fat thermometer registers 375 degrees.
5. While oil is heating, line platter with double thickness of paper towels; set aside.
6. Blot tortillas with paper towels to absorb any excess moisture and cut each tortilla into quarters.
7. Using mesh strainer or slotted spatula, carefully lower about half the tortilla triangles into the hot oil and fry, turning once with tongs, 1 to 2 minutes, or until crisp.
8. Transfer triangles to paper-towel-lined platter to drain. Repeat with remaining triangles.
9. Arrange tortilla chips, cheese, jícama, chilies, and coriander if desired, decoratively on serving platter and set aside until ready to serve.

Mazatlán Sopa Seca

Medium-size onion
2 medium-size tomatoes
4-ounce can diced mild green Anaheim chilies
1 pound medium-size shrimp
3 tablespoons vegetable oil
8 ounces vermicelli
1 clove garlic, crushed and peeled
2 cups chicken stock
Salt and freshly ground pepper
8-ounce container sour cream (optional)
1 tablespoon chopped coriander

1. Halve, peel, and chop enough onion to measure 1 cup.
2. Wash and dry tomatoes. Core, halve, and seed tomatoes. Chop enough to measure 1½ cups; set aside.
3. Turn chilies into strainer and rinse under cold running water; set aside to drain.
4. Pinch off legs of shrimp, several at a time, then bend back and snap off sharp, beaklike piece of shell just above tail. Remove shell and discard. Using sharp paring knife, make shallow incision along back of each shrimp, exposing black digestive vein. Extract black vein and discard. (See following illustration.)
5. Rinse shrimp in colander and set aside to drain.
6. Heat oil in large heavy-gauge skillet over medium-high heat.
7. While oil is heating, break vermicelli into 1- to 1½-inch-long pieces. Add vermicelli to hot oil and sauté, stirring continuously to prevent burning, 1 to 2 minutes, or until golden.
8. Drain off any excess oil from pan. Add onion, tomatoes, chilies, and garlic, and stir to combine.

9. Add stock, and salt and pepper to taste. Reduce heat to low, cover pan, and cook 15 minutes.
10. Pat shrimp dry with paper towels. Add shrimp to pan and stir to combine. Cook 2 to 3 minutes, or until shrimp begin to curl and backs turn opaque.
11. Meanwhile, if using sour cream, turn into small serving bowl and set aside.
12. Turn sopa seca into large serving dish and sprinkle with chopped coriander. Serve with sour cream on the side, if desired.

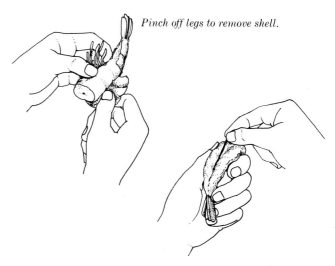

Pinch off legs to remove shell.

Extract digestive vein with your fingers.

Tossed Salad

Small head romaine lettuce
Medium-size red bell pepper
5¾-ounce can pitted black olives
1 cup frozen corn kernels, thawed
Large lemon
⅓ cup olive oil
2 teaspoons prepared mustard
1 clove garlic, crushed and peeled
Salt and freshly ground pepper

1. Wash romaine and dry in salad spinner or with paper towels. Remove and discard any bruised or discolored leaves. Tear romaine into bite-size pieces and place in salad bowl; set aside.
2. Wash bell pepper and dry with paper towel. Halve, core, and seed pepper. Cut pepper into 1-inch squares and add to salad bowl.
3. Drain olives and add to salad bowl.
4. Pat corn dry with paper towels and add to salad bowl. Cover bowl with plastic wrap and refrigerate until ready to serve.
5. Squeeze enough lemon juice to measure 2 tablespoons.
6. For dressing, combine lemon juice, olive oil, mustard, garlic, and salt and pepper to taste in small nonaluminum bowl and whisk until blended; set aside.
7. Just before serving, whisk dressing to recombine and pour over salad. Toss salad until evenly coated and serve.

Guacamole Salad
Chicken Burritos with Mexican Rice and Salsa Cruda

Introduce your children to Mexican food with this traditional meal of chicken burritos, *guacamole salad, and* salsa cruda.

Also called *tomates verdes, tomatillos* look like small green tomatoes and are just as tart. Canned *tomatillos* are sold in the Mexican food section of many supermarkets. Store any unused *tomatillos* in a covered container in the refrigerator for up to five days.

To make the *burritos,* you will need flour tortillas, the staple bread of northern Mexico. Made from wheat flour, lard or shortening, salt, and water, flour tortillas are generally larger than corn tortillas and are ideal for folding around fillings.

In Mexico, *burritos* are commonly served with a *salsa,* such as this one of tomatoes, onion, and chilies. Here the cook uses mild Anaheim, or California, green chilies, which are readily available canned. If you prefer a more piquant sauce, substitute fresh *serrano* chilies, very small fiery-hot chilies sold in Mexican groceries.

SHOPPING LIST AND STAPLES

2 whole boneless, skinless chicken breasts, halved (about 1½ pounds total weight)
2 large ripe avocados
6 small tomatoes (1½ to 2 pounds total weight)
1 head red leaf lettuce
Small green bell pepper
Small red bell pepper
2 or 3 fresh mild green Anaheim chilies, or 4-ounce can
1 or 2 fresh jalapeño or serrano chilies, or 4-ounce can
3 medium-size yellow onions
Small red onion
Small bunch scallions (optional)
8 cloves garlic
Small bunch coriander
2 limes
¼ pound Monterey Jack cheese
4 fresh 10- to 12-inch flour tortillas, or 1 package frozen
2 cups chicken stock, preferably homemade (see page 12), or canned
13-ounce can tomatillos
4-ounce can diced mild green chilies
4-ounce jar whole pimientos (optional)
2 tablespoons vegetable oil
1 cup long-grain rice
½ teaspoon chili powder
¼ teaspoon ground cumin
Pinch of sugar
Salt and freshly ground pepper

UTENSILS

Food processor or blender
Medium-size heavy-gauge sauté pan with cover
Medium-size heavy-gauge saucepan
Small saucepan
Small heatproof bowl
Strainer
Measuring cups and spoons
Chef's knife

Paring knife
Wooden spoon
Rubber spatula
Grater (if not using processor)
Rubber gloves (if using fresh chilies)

START-TO-FINISH STEPS

One hour ahead: If using frozen tortillas for burritos recipe, set out to thaw.

1. Wash and dry coriander. Trim stem ends and discard. Measure ¼ cup loosely packed sprigs for salsa recipe; set aside. Set aside 4 sprigs if using for guacamole garnish and coarsely chop enough remaining coriander to measure 2 tablespoons for guacamole recipe. Under flat blade of chef's knife, crush garlic for guacamole, rice, and salsa recipes; remove peels and discard. Peel and mince enough remaining garlic to measure 1 tablespoon for burritos recipe. Halve and peel red and yellow onions. Coarsely chop enough red onion to measure ½ cup for guacamole recipe; reserve remainder for another use. Coarsely chop enough yellow onion to measure 1 cup for burritos recipe, 1 cup for rice recipe, and ½ cup for salsa recipe; set aside. Wash tomatoes and dry with paper towels. Core, halve, and seed tomatoes. Chop 2 tomatoes for burritos recipe and quarter remaining 4 tomatoes for salsa recipe.
2. Follow salsa recipe steps 1 through 3.
3. Follow rice recipe steps 1 through 7 and burritos recipe steps 1 and 2.
4. Follow rice recipe step 8 and burritos recipe steps 3 and 4.
5. While chicken filling and rice simmer, follow guacamole recipe steps 1 through 5 and burritos recipe step 5.
6. While tortillas are warming, follow guacamole recipe steps 6 through 8.
7. Follow rice recipe step 9, burritos recipe steps 6 through 8, and serve with guacamole.

RECIPES

Guacamole Salad

1 to 2 fresh jalapeño or serrano chilies, or 4-ounce can
2 limes
13-ounce can tomatillos
2 large ripe avocados
½ cup coarsely chopped red onion
1 to 2 cloves garlic, crushed and peeled
2 tablespoons coarsely chopped coriander, plus 4 sprigs for garnish (optional)
Salt and freshly ground pepper
4-ounce jar whole pimientos for garnish (optional)
1 head red leaf lettuce

1. Wearing rubber gloves, rinse fresh chilies, if using, under cold running water and dry with paper towels. Trim stems and discard. Coarsely chop enough chilies to measure 1 to 2 tablespoons. If using canned chilies, turn into strainer, rinse under cold running water, and dry with paper towels. Proceed as for fresh chilies.

2. Squeeze enough lime juice to measure 2 tablespoons; set aside.

3. Drain enough tomatillos to measure ½ cup; set aside.

4. Halve avocados lengthwise, cutting around and under pits. Twist halves in opposite directions to separate. Remove and discard pits. Using metal spoon, scoop out flesh and place in container of food processor or blender.

5. Add chilies, lime juice, tomatillos, onion, garlic, chopped coriander, and salt and pepper to taste to avocados and turn machine on and off a few times until mixture is blended but not smooth; set aside.

6. If using pimientos, turn into strainer and rinse under cold running water. Drain, dry, and set aside.

7. Wash and dry lettuce. Remove and discard any bruised or discolored leaves. Using 2 or 3 leaves for each, form small beds for guacamole on 4 dinner plates.

8. Top lettuce with equal portions of guacamole and garnish each serving with a pimiento and a sprig of coriander, if desired.

Chicken Burritos with Mexican Rice and Salsa Cruda

2 whole boneless, skinless chicken breasts, halved
   (about 1½ pounds total weight)
4-ounce can diced mild green chilies
1 cup coarsely chopped yellow onion
1 tablespoon minced garlic
2 small tomatoes, seeded and chopped
Salt and freshly ground pepper
4 fresh 10- to 12-inch flour tortillas, or 4 frozen tortillas,
   thawed
¼ pound Monterey Jack cheese
Mexican Rice (see following recipe)
Salsa Cruda (see following recipe)

1. Preheat oven to 350 degrees.

2. Rinse chicken under cold running water and dry with paper towels. Cut each breast half into 3-inch-long by ½-inch-wide strips.

3. Turn chilies into strainer and rinse under cold running water. Drain and dry with paper towels.

4. Combine chicken strips, chilies, onion, garlic, and tomatoes in medium-size heavy-gauge saucepan. Season with salt and pepper, and bring to a simmer over medium-high heat. Reduce heat and simmer gently 15 to 25 minutes, or until chicken is fork-tender.

5. Stack tortillas and wrap tightly in heavy-duty foil. Place on middle rack of oven and warm 10 minutes.

6. Using food processor fitted with shredding disk, or grater, grate cheese; set aside.

7. Divide warm tortillas among 4 dinner plates.

8. Remove chicken filling from heat. Taste and adjust seasoning. Top tortillas with equal portions of chicken filling and rice, sprinkle each serving with cheese, and serve with salsa cruda on the side.

Mexican Rice

1 cup coarsely chopped yellow onion
2 cloves garlic, crushed and peeled
½ teaspoon chili powder
¼ teaspoon ground cumin
1 cup long-grain rice
1 each small red and green bell pepper
Small bunch scallions (optional)
2 tablespoons vegetable oil
2 cups chicken stock
Salt and freshly ground pepper

1. Bring 2 cups cold water to a boil in small saucepan over high heat.

2. Meanwhile, combine onion, garlic, chili powder, and cumin in food processor or blender and process about 30 seconds, or just until smooth; set aside.

3. Place rice in small heatproof bowl and cover with boiling water; set aside 10 minutes.

4. Meanwhile, wash bell peppers and dry with paper towels. Halve, core, and seed peppers. Dice enough red and green pepper to measure ½ cup each; set aside.

5. Wash and dry scallions, if using. Trim ends and discard. Chop enough scallions to measure ¼ cup; set aside. Reserve remaining scallions for another use.

6. Heat oil in medium-size heavy-gauge sauté pan over medium-high heat.

7. Meanwhile, turn rice into strainer and drain thoroughly. Add rice to hot oil and sauté, stirring occasionally, about 5 minutes, or until golden.

8. Stir in chicken stock, onion-spice mixture, and salt and pepper to taste, and bring to a boil. Cover pan, reduce heat, and simmer gently, stirring occasionally, about 20 minutes, or until liquid is absorbed.

9. Remove rice from heat, add diced peppers, and scallions if desired, and toss with fork to combine.

Salsa Cruda

2 to 3 fresh mild green Anaheim chilies, or 4-ounce can
4 small tomatoes, cored and quartered
½ cup coarsely chopped yellow onion
1 to 2 cloves garlic, crushed and peeled
¼ cup loosely packed coriander sprigs
Pinch of sugar
Salt and freshly ground pepper

1. Wearing rubber gloves, rinse fresh chilies, if using, under cold running water and dry with paper towels. Trim stems and discard. Coarsely chop enough chilies to measure ¼ cup. If using canned chilies, turn into strainer, rinse under cold running water, and dry with paper towels. Proceed as for fresh chilies.

2. Combine chilies, tomatoes, onion, garlic, coriander, sugar, and salt and pepper to taste in food processor or blender and turn machine on and off 2 or 3 times until mixture is chunky, not smooth. Do *not* overprocess.

3. Turn salsa cruda into serving bowl and set aside for at least 30 minutes before serving.

Tortilla Soup
Beef Tacos with Green Salsa
Confetti Vegetables

Tortilla soup, a beef taco with salsa, *and vegetable salad are color-complemented by an earth-toned table setting.*

Pequín chilies are a suggested flavoring for both the tortilla soup and the confetti vegetables. These tiny, bright red chilies, which are even hotter than *serranos*, are available in Mexican groceries and some southwestern supermarkets. If you cannot find them, substitute ¼ teaspoon of ground Cayenne pepper for one crushed *pequín* chili.

SHOPPING LIST AND STAPLES

¾ pound ground beef
1 pound Swiss chard or spinach

2 medium-size ripe avocados
½ pint cherry tomatoes
Small head romaine lettuce
2 medium-size onions
Small bunch scallions
1 or 2 fresh jalapeño or serrano chilies (optional)
3 cloves garlic
Small bunch coriander
2 lemons
8-ounce container sour cream (optional)
¼ pound sharp Cheddar cheese
¼ pound Monterey Jack cheese

¼ pound Parmesan cheese
10 fresh corn tortillas, or 1 package frozen
4½ cups beef stock, preferably homemade (see page 12), or canned
15½-ounce can chickpeas
13-ounce can tomatillos
6-ounce can tomato paste
10-ounce package frozen corn kernels
2⅓ cups vegetable oil
4 dried pequín chilies plus 4 additional pequín chilies (optional)
1 teaspoon ground cumin
Salt
Freshly ground pepper

UTENSILS

Food processor or blender
Large heavy-gauge skillet with cover
Medium-size skillet
2 medium-size saucepans, 1 heavy-gauge
3 small bowls
Salad spinner (optional)
Large strainer
Measuring cups and spoons
Chef's knife
Paring knife
Wooden spoon
Slotted spatula
Rubber spatula
Deep-fat thermometer
Citrus juicer (optional)
Grater (if not using processor)
Mortar and pestle (optional)
Rolling pin (if not using mortar and pestle)
Rubber gloves (if using fresh chilies)

START-TO-FINISH STEPS

One hour ahead: Set out frozen corn kernels, and frozen tortillas if using, to thaw for vegetables and tacos recipes.

1. Peel and quarter 1 onion for salsa recipe and halve, peel, and chop enough remaining onion to measure ¾ cup for vegetables recipe. Peel and mince 2 cloves garlic for vegetables recipe and 1 clove for tacos recipe. Squeeze enough lemon juice to measure 2 tablespoons each for soup recipe and tacos recipe. Using food processor fitted with steel blade, or grater, grate enough Parmesan to measure ¾ cup for vegetables recipe. Transfer to small serving bowl; set aside. Using food processor fitted with shredding disk, or grater, shred Monterey Jack cheese for soup recipe and Cheddar for tacos recipe; you should have 1 cup of each.
2. Follow salsa recipe steps 1 through 5.
3. Follow tacos recipe steps 1 through 4.
4. Follow soup recipe steps 1 through 6.
5. Follow vegetables recipe steps 1 through 7.
6. While vegetables are cooking, follow tacos recipe steps 5 through 7 and soup recipe step 7.

7. Follow tacos recipe steps 8 and 9, vegetables recipe step 8, soup recipe step 8, and serve.

RECIPES

Tortilla Soup

2 cherry tomatoes
Medium-size ripe avocado
2 tablespoons freshly squeezed lemon juice
2 cups vegetable oil
2 fresh corn tortillas, or 2 frozen corn tortillas, thawed
4½ cups beef stock
1 cup shredded Monterey Jack cheese
4 dried pequín chilies (optional)

1. Wash cherry tomatoes and dry with paper towels. Remove stems, if necessary, and discard. Halve tomatoes through stem end; set aside.
2. Halve avocado lengthwise, cutting around and under pit. Twist halves in opposite directions to separate. Remove pit and discard. Peel one half and cut crosswise into 8 slices. Place slices on plate, sprinkle with lemon juice to prevent discoloration, and turn to coat evenly; set aside. Reserve remaining avocado half for another use.
3. Heat oil in medium-size heavy-gauge saucepan over medium-high heat until deep-fat thermometer registers 375 degrees.
4. Meanwhile, line plate with double thickness of paper towels; set aside.
5. Blot tortillas with paper towels to absorb any excess moisture and cut into 1-inch-wide strips. Using slotted spatula, carefully lower strips into hot oil and fry 45 seconds, or until crisp.
6. Transfer tortilla strips to towel-lined plate to drain.
7. Bring stock to a simmer in another medium-size saucepan over medium-high heat.
8. Divide cherry tomato halves, avocado slices, tortilla strips, shredded cheese, and chilies if using, among 4 large soup bowls. Pour hot stock into bowls and serve.

Beef Tacos with Green Salsa

Small bunch scallions
Medium-size ripe avocado
2 tablespoons freshly squeezed lemon juice
Small head romaine lettuce
8 fresh corn tortillas, or 8 frozen corn tortillas, thawed
¾ pound ground beef
1 clove garlic, peeled and minced
1 teaspoon ground cumin
Salt
Freshly ground pepper
1 cup shredded sharp Cheddar cheese
Green Salsa (see following recipe)
8-ounce container sour cream (optional)

1. Wash scallions under cold running water and dry with paper towels. Trim ends and discard. Chop enough scal-

lions to measure 1 cup; set aside.

2. Halve avocado lengthwise, cutting around and under pit. Twist halves in opposite directions to separate. Remove and discard pit. Peel avocado, cut into ½-inch dice, and place in small bowl. Sprinkle with lemon juice to prevent discoloration and toss gently until evenly coated; set aside.

3. Wash lettuce and dry in salad spinner or with paper towels. Remove and discard any bruised or discolored leaves. Stack several leaves, fold in half lengthwise, and cut enough lettuce crosswise into ¼-inch shreds to measure 1 cup. Reserve remaining lettuce for another use.

4. Preheat oven to 350 degrees.

5. Stack tortillas in piles of 4 each and wrap tightly in heavy-duty foil. Place on middle rack of oven to warm about 10 minutes.

6. Meanwhile, cook ground beef in medium-size skillet over medium-high heat, stirring and breaking up lumps with fork, 3 to 4 minutes, or until browned.

7. Add minced garlic, cumin, and salt and pepper to taste, and stir to combine. Remove skillet from heat and set aside.

8. Remove tortillas from oven and unwrap. Working quickly, hold 2 overlapping tortillas in one hand and fill tortillas with one quarter of beef mixture, chopped scallions, diced avocado, shredded lettuce, and shredded cheese. Roll closed and transfer to dinner plate. Repeat with remaining tortillas and filling ingredients.

9. Top each taco with salsa, and a dollop of sour cream if desired, and serve with extra salsa on the side.

Green Salsa

1 to 2 fresh jalapeño or serrano chilies (optional)
13-ounce can tomatillos
Small bunch coriander
Medium-size onion, peeled and quartered
2 tablespoons vegetable oil
Salt
Freshly ground pepper

1. Wearing rubber gloves, rinse fresh chilies, if using, and dry with paper towels. Trim stem ends and discard. Chop chilies coarsely; set aside.

2. Drain tomatillos.

3. Wash coriander and dry with paper towels. Trim stem ends and discard. Measure ⅓ cup loosely packed sprigs and set aside. Reserve remaining coriander for another use.

4. Combine chilies, tomatillos, coriander, onion, oil, and salt and pepper to taste in food processor fitted with steel blade, or in blender, and process until smooth.

5. Turn salsa into small bowl and set aside.

Confetti Vegetables

1 pound Swiss chard or spinach
4 dried pequín chilies (optional)
10-ounce package frozen corn kernels, thawed
15½-ounce can chickpeas
3 tablespoons vegetable oil
¾ cup chopped onion
2 cloves garlic, peeled and minced
3 tablespoons tomato paste
Salt and freshly ground pepper
¾ cup freshly grated Parmesan cheese

1. Wash Swiss chard or spinach thoroughly in several changes of cold water; do *not* dry. Trim stem ends and discard. Coarsely chop leaves; set aside.

2. Crush enough chilies, if using, in mortar with pestle to measure ½ teaspoon. Or, place chilies between 2 sheets of waxed paper and crush with rolling pin. Set aside.

3. Turn corn into small bowl and pat dry with paper towels; set aside.

4. Turn chickpeas into large strainer and rinse under cold running water; set aside to drain.

5. Heat oil in large heavy-gauge skillet over medium-high heat. Add onion and garlic and sauté, stirring, 1 to 2 minutes.

6. Add Swiss chard or spinach and sauté, stirring occasionally, 5 minutes.

7. Drain off all but 2 tablespoons liquid from skillet. Stir in crushed chilies, chickpeas, corn, tomato paste, and salt and pepper to taste. Cover skillet, reduce heat to low, and cook gently about 10 minutes.

8. Divide vegetables among 4 dinner plates and sprinkle each serving with 1 tablespoon grated Parmesan. Serve remaining Parmesan on the side.

ADDED TOUCH

Polvorones are sugar-coated shortbread-like treats that literally melt in the mouth. These cookies may be made with an electric mixer, but the traditional method is by hand.

Polvorones

4 sticks unsalted butter, at room temperature
3 to 3½ cups all-purpose flour
¾ cup confectioners' sugar
Pinch of salt
1 tablespoon vanilla extract
1 cup finely chopped almonds or pecans

1. Preheat oven to 350 degrees.

2. Lightly grease cookie sheet; set aside.

3. Cut butter into 1-tablespoon pieces.

4. Combine butter, flour, ½ cup confectioners' sugar, salt, vanilla, and nuts in large mixing bowl and, working quickly, stir with wooden spoon until blended. Dough will be fairly stiff.

5. Roll heaping teaspoonsful of dough into small balls and place about 2 inches apart on prepared sheet. Bake 20 to 25 minutes, or until cookies turn pale golden.

6. Dredge cookies immediately with remaining confectioners' sugar and transfer to serving platter. Yields 6 dozen cookies.

Kathleen Kenny Sanderson

H aving cooked for her eight siblings for many years, Kathleen Kenny Sanderson long ago learned a simple rule for pleasing the majority at dinner: Avoid exotic or overly spiced foods. This does not mean that foreign or regional American cuisines are taboo, however, as her three menus show. In each, she uses beef—America's best-selling meat—in a different way.

In Menu 1, the entrée is a toned-down version of the often fiery southwestern favorite, chili. Here the cook combines ground beef with kidney beans, onion, and tomatoes, and lightly spices the mixture with chili powder and hot pepper sauce to taste. Hot corn sticks with honey butter and coleslaw made with red and green cabbage are the down-home accompaniments.

Ground beef is again prominent in Menu 3, this time in a fancy meat loaf filled with Provolone cheese and topped with a light tomato sauce. Kathleen Sanderson complements the entrée with home-style potato pancakes, which resemble hashbrowns in texture and taste.

Chinese cooking inspires Menu 2, in which the two main dishes are stir fried: Strips of steak cook quickly with broccoli, cherry tomatoes, carrots, and ginger; and white rice is tossed with eggs, vegetables, and ham if desired. The fried rice can easily become a meal in itself when additional meat and vegetables are included.

Serve the beef-and-bean chili sprinkled with grated Cheddar from a large tureen and the hot corn sticks from a basket with honey butter on the side. The festive slaw is tossed with a light caraway-flavored dressing.

Quick Chili with Cheese
Red and Green Slaw
Corn Sticks with Honey Butter

The cook prefers dark red kidney beans for this chili because they hold their shape and color better than pink beans or pinto beans. For a more traditional dish, use diced flank or skirt steak instead of ground beef, and offer sour cream, chopped scallions, diced mild green chilies, and crumbled taco chips, in addition to the grated cheese, for toppings.

When baked in a corn-stick mold, the corn bread resembles little ears of corn. Cast-iron corn-stick molds are readily available at kitchen supply stores and should be well seasoned before use. Coating the mold with butter before baking ensures that the sticks develop a crisp crust. If you do not have a corn-stick mold, use a 12-cup muffin pan and bake the breads the same way.

SHOPPING LIST AND STAPLES

1½ pounds ground beef chuck
Small head red cabbage (about 1 pound)
Small head green cabbage (about 1 pound)
2 large carrots (about ½ pound total weight)
Large yellow onion
2 large eggs
1 cup milk
1 stick unsalted butter
⅓ pound Cheddar cheese
35-ounce can imported plum tomatoes
6-ounce can tomato paste
15-ounce can dark red kidney beans
1 cup plus 1 tablespoon vegetable oil
¼ cup white wine vinegar or distilled vinegar
1 tablespoon Dijon mustard
Hot pepper sauce
3 tablespoons honey
1 cup all-purpose flour
1 cup cornmeal
¼ cup sugar
3 teaspoons baking powder
2 tablespoons chili powder
1 teaspoon cinnamon
½ teaspoon caraway seeds
Salt and freshly ground pepper

UTENSILS

Food processor (optional)
Dutch oven or large, deep heavy-gauge skillet

12-stick corn-stick mold
2 medium-size bowls
2 small bowls, 1 nonaluminum
Strainer
Measuring cups and spoons
Chef's knife
Paring knife
2 wooden spoons
Rubber spatula
Whisk
Grater (if not using processor)

START-TO-FINISH STEPS

Thirty minutes ahead: Set out butter to come to room temperature for corn-stick recipe.

1. Follow chili recipe steps 1 through 5.
2. While chili simmers, follow slaw recipe steps 1 through 6.
3. Follow chili recipe steps 6 and 7.
4. Follow corn-stick recipe steps 1 through 9.
5. Follow chili recipe steps 8 and 9, corn-stick recipe step 10, and serve with slaw.

RECIPES

Quick Chili with Cheese

Large yellow onion
1 tablespoon vegetable oil
1½ pounds ground beef chuck
35-ounce can imported plum tomatoes
6 tablespoons tomato paste
15-ounce can dark red kidney beans
2 tablespoons chili powder
Hot pepper sauce
Salt and freshly ground pepper
⅓ pound Cheddar cheese

1. Peel and chop enough onion to measure 1½ cups.
2. Heat oil in Dutch oven or large, deep heavy-gauge skillet over medium-high heat. Add ground beef and sauté, stirring and breaking up lumps with side of spoon, 3 to 4 minutes, or until browned.
3. Drain off fat and excess oil from meat. Raise heat to high, add chopped onion, and cook, stirring frequently, 3 to 5 minutes.
4. Stir in tomatoes with their juice and bring to a boil.

5. Add tomato paste and stir until blended. Reduce heat and simmer gently, uncovered, 20 minutes.

6. Turn kidney beans into strainer and rinse under cold running water. Set aside to drain.

7. Add kidney beans, chili powder, and hot pepper sauce, salt, and pepper to taste to meat mixture; stir to combine and simmer, uncovered, another 20 minutes.

8. Using food processor or grater, shred Cheddar.

9. Turn chili into large serving bowl, top with grated Cheddar, and serve.

Red and Green Slaw

Small head green cabbage (about 1 pound)
Small head red cabbage (about 1 pound)
2 large carrots (about ½ pound total weight)
Large egg
1 tablespoon Dijon mustard
¼ cup white wine vinegar or distilled vinegar
½ teaspoon caraway seeds
¾ cup vegetable oil
Salt and freshly ground pepper

1. Halve each head of cabbage lengthwise. Remove core from one half green cabbage and one half red cabbage and discard; reserve remaining cabbage halves for another use. If using processor fitted with shredding disk, cut cored cabbages to fit feed tube and shred enough to measure 8 cups. Or, shred cabbage on coarse side of grater. Transfer cabbage to large serving bowl or platter.

2. Peel and trim carrots. Using food processor fitted with grating disk, or grater, grate enough carrots to measure 1¼ cups. Add grated carrots to cabbage and toss to combine; set aside.

3. For dressing, separate egg, placing yolk in small non-aluminum bowl and reserving white for another use. Whisk yolk until smooth.

4. Add mustard, vinegar, and caraway seeds, and whisk until blended.

5. Whisking continuously, add oil in a slow steady stream and whisk until thick and smooth. Season with salt and pepper to taste.

6. Pour dressing over slaw and toss until evenly coated. Cover and set aside at room temperature for at least 20 minutes before serving.

Corn Sticks with Honey Butter

1 cup cornmeal
1 cup all-purpose flour
3 teaspoons baking powder
¼ teaspoon salt
Large egg
1 cup milk
¼ cup sugar
¼ cup vegetable oil
1 stick unsalted butter, at room temperature
3 tablespoons honey
1 teaspoon cinnamon

1. Preheat oven to 425 degrees.

2. Grease corn-stick mold; set aside.

3. Combine cornmeal, flour, baking powder, and salt in medium-size bowl and stir with fork to blend.

4. Combine egg and milk in another medium-size bowl and whisk until blended. Whisk in sugar. Add oil and whisk until blended.

5. Fold dry ingredients into egg mixture and beat vigorously (20 strokes); batter will be slightly lumpy.

6. Spoon batter into prepared mold and bake 20 minutes, or until corn sticks are lightly browned.

7. Meanwhile, cream butter in small bowl.

8. Add honey and cinnamon, and stir until well blended.

9. Turn honey butter into small serving bowl or ramekin; set aside until ready to serve.

10. Turn corn sticks into napkin-lined basket and serve with honey butter.

ADDED TOUCH

These sinfully rich, moist brownies are best if made the day before you plan to serve them; they firm up when cool and have a cheesecake-like texture.

Reva's Rich Brownies

1½ cups walnut pieces
2 sticks unsalted butter, at room temperature
2 cups granulated sugar
4 eggs, at room temperature
¼ teaspoon salt
1 cup cocoa powder
1 cup all-purpose flour

Filling:
8-ounce package cream cheese, at room temperature
⅓ cup granulated sugar
1¼ teaspoons vanilla extract
1 egg, at room temperature

1. Preheat oven to 350 degrees.

2. Grease and flour 13 x 9 x 2-inch baking pan and set aside.

3. Coarsely chop nuts; set aside.

4. Using wooden spoon or mixer, cream butter and sugar in large mixing bowl; set aside.

5. Add eggs and salt, and beat until light and fluffy.

6. Add cocoa and nuts, and mix until well blended.

7. Add flour and beat until totally incorporated; set aside.

8. Combine filling ingredients in small bowl and stir until well blended; set aside.

9. Turn half of brownie batter into prepared pan and, using rubber spatula, spread evenly over bottom of pan. Add filling and spread evenly over brownie layer. Top with remaining brownie batter and swirl knife through mixture to create marbled effect.

10. Bake brownies 35 minutes, or until toothpick inserted in center comes out clean.

11. When brownies are done, transfer pan to wire rack to cool. Cut brownies into 2-inch squares and serve.

Stir-Fried Flank Steak and Vegetables
Fried Rice in Lettuce Cups

Offer Oriental food fans two tempting stir-fried dishes—beef with vegetables, and rice with ham and peas in lettuce cups.

This simple stir-fried entrée of steak strips and vegetables is a delightfully quick and colorful meal. You can substitute pork loin, or any other lean meat—or shrimp, scallops, or chicken—for the steak.

For perfect fried rice, be certain the rice is completely dry and preferably cooled, otherwise it will clump and absorb too much oil. Chilled leftover rice is also good for frying.

SHOPPING LIST AND STAPLES

1½ pounds lean beef flank steak
¼ pound boiled ham (optional)
1 bunch broccoli (about 1¾ pounds)
3 large carrots (about ¾ pound total weight)
½ pint cherry tomatoes
1 head Bibb lettuce
Small bunch scallions
2-inch piece fresh ginger
2 eggs
10-ounce package frozen peas

3 cups chicken stock, preferably homemade (see page 12), or canned (optional)
½ cup peanut oil
½ cup soy sauce
1½ cups long-grain rice
Salt

UTENSILS

Wok or Dutch oven with cover
Medium-size heavy-gauge saucepan with cover
Jelly-roll pan
Medium-size heatproof bowl
Small bowl
Measuring cups and spoons
Chef's knife
Paring knife
Wok spatula or wooden spoon
Vegetable peeler
Grater

88

START-TO-FINISH STEPS

One hour ahead: Set out frozen peas to thaw for rice recipe.

1. Follow rice recipe step 1.
2. While rice simmers, follow steak recipe steps 1 through 5.
3. Follow rice recipe steps 2 through 15.
4. Follow steak recipe steps 6 through 9, rice recipe step 16, and serve.

RECIPES

Stir-Fried Flank Steak and Vegetables

1 bunch broccoli (about 1¾ pounds)
10 cherry tomatoes
3 large carrots (about ¾ pound total weight)
2-inch piece fresh ginger
1½ pounds lean beef flank steak
¼ cup peanut oil
¼ cup soy sauce

1. Wash broccoli and dry with paper towels. Trim stems and reserve for another use. Cut enough broccoli tops into florets to measure 3 cups; set aside.
2. Wash and dry tomatoes. Remove stems, if necessary, and discard. Halve tomatoes through stem end.
3. Peel and trim carrots. Cut each carrot crosswise on diagonal into ¼-inch-thick pieces; set aside.
4. Peel ginger; using grater, grate enough to measure 2 tablespoons.
5. Cut flank steak into 2-inch-long by ¼-inch-wide strips.
6. Heat wok or Dutch oven over high heat. Add oil and tilt and rotate pan to coat sides. When oil is hot enough to evaporate a drop of water on contact, add steak and stir fry until evenly coated with oil. Cook 2 to 3 minutes.
7. Add vegetables and stir fry 2 to 3 minutes.
8. Reduce heat to medium, add ginger and soy sauce, and toss to combine. Cover pan and cook 1 minute.
9. Divide steak and vegetables among 4 dinner plates and serve.

Fried Rice in Lettuce Cups

3 tablespoons peanut oil
1½ cups long-grain rice
3 cups chicken stock (optional)
½ teaspoon salt (if not using stock)
Small bunch scallions
¼ pound boiled ham (optional)
2 eggs
1 cup frozen peas, thawed
¼ cup soy sauce
1 head Bibb lettuce

1. Heat 1 tablespoon oil in medium-size heavy-gauge saucepan over medium heat. Add rice and stir until evenly coated with oil. Stir in stock or 3 cups water and bring to a boil over high heat. If not using stock, add salt. Cover pan, reduce heat to low, and simmer rice gently, undisturbed, 15 to 18 minutes, or until liquid is absorbed.
2. Remove rice from heat and fluff with fork; spread out on jelly-roll pan, and place in freezer for about 5 minutes to cool.
3. Meanwhile, preheat oven to 200 degrees.
4. Wash scallions and dry with paper towels. Trim ends and discard. Chop enough scallions to measure ½ cup; reserve remainder for another use.
5. If using ham, cut enough into ¼-inch dice to measure ¾ cup; set aside.
6. Heat wok or Dutch oven over medium-high heat.
7. While pan is heating, crack eggs into small bowl, add scallions, and beat with fork just until blended.
8. Add 1 tablespoon oil to pan and tilt and rotate pan to coat sides. When oil is hot enough to evaporate a drop of water on contact, add egg and scallion mixture, and scramble. Turn eggs out onto plate and set aside. Wipe out pan.
9. Return pan to medium-high heat. Add remaining oil and tilt and rotate pan to coat sides. When oil is hot, add cooked rice and stir fry 2 to 3 minutes.
10. Add peas and stir fry 1 minute, or until heated through.
11. Add scrambled eggs and stir fry, breaking up eggs with edge of wok spatula or wooden spoon, 1 minute.
12. Add diced ham and toss to combine.
13. Add soy sauce and toss until rice is evenly coated.
14. Turn rice into medium-size heatproof bowl, cover loosely with foil, and keep warm in oven until ready to serve.
15. Meanwhile, wash and dry lettuce. Remove and discard any bruised or discolored leaves. Place two whole leaves on each of 4 dinner plates; set aside. Reserve remaining lettuce for another use.
16. Just before serving, remove rice from oven, divide among lettuce cups, and serve.

Cheese Meat Loaf with Tomato Sauce
Potato Pancakes

For a quick and filling weekday dinner, serve the family ample slices of Provolone-filled meat loaf topped with freshly made tomato sauce, and crusty golden potato pancakes flavored with scallions.

The tasty rolled meat loaf is filled with Provolone cheese. For variety, fill the loaf with a combination of shredded or grated cheeses, or add chopped blanched vegetables to the filling. When rolling the meat loaf, be sure to enclose the cheese completely so it does not leak out as it melts. Before cutting, let the loaf cool slightly to allow the cheese to firm. The meat loaf is topped with a versatile tomato sauce that can be used on pasta or seafood.

Crispy potato pancakes are foolproof if you use thoroughly dried shreds from a high-starch potato variety such as Russet. Because any excess moisture in the potatoes makes the batter too thin and causes the hot fat to splatter, wring the potatoes dry in a kitchen towel, working quickly because the potatoes darken when exposed to air. You can grate the potatoes ahead of time, cover them with acidulated water, and refrigerate until ready to use.

SHOPPING LIST AND STAPLES

1½ pounds ground beef chuck
1½ pounds Russet potatoes
Small bunch scallions
Small onion
1 clove garlic
Small bunch parsley
3 eggs
½ cup milk
¼ pound sliced Provolone cheese
25-ounce can crushed tomatoes
2 tablespoons olive oil
2 tablespoons vegetable oil, approximately
⅓ cup dry unseasoned bread crumbs
3 tablespoons all-purpose flour
½ teaspoon dried oregano
½ teaspoon dried basil
Salt and freshly ground pepper

UTENSILS

Food processor (optional)
Large cast-iron skillet or griddle
Medium-size heavy-gauge saucepan with cover
13 x 9 x 2-inch baking dish
Heatproof platter
Large nonaluminum bowl
2 medium-size bowls

Colander
Measuring cups and spoons
Chef's knife
Paring knife
Wooden spoon
Metal spatula
Whisk
Grater (if not using food processor)
Vegetable peeler

START-TO-FINISH STEPS

1. Wash and dry parsley. Trim stem ends and discard. Set aside 4 sprigs for garnish for meat loaf recipe, if desired, and chop enough parsley to measure 2 tablespoons for sauce recipe. Reserve remainder for another use.
2. Follow meat loaf recipe steps 1 through 7.
3. While meat loaf is baking, follow potato pancakes recipe steps 1 through 4.
4. Follow sauce recipe steps 1 through 5.
5. While sauce simmers, follow potato pancakes recipe steps 5 through 9.
6. Follow meat loaf recipe step 8 and reduce oven temperature to 200 degrees. Follow sauce recipe step 6.
7. While meat loaf is resting, follow potato pancakes recipe step 10.
8. Follow meat loaf recipe step 9 and serve with potato pancakes.

RECIPES

Cheese Meat Loaf with Tomato Sauce

1½ pounds ground beef chuck
1 egg
⅓ cup dry unseasoned bread crumbs
½ teaspoon dried oregano
½ teaspoon dried basil
Salt and freshly ground pepper
6 slices Provolone cheese
Tomato Sauce (see following recipe)
4 sprigs parsley for garnish (optional)

1. Preheat oven to 375 degrees.
2. Line 13 x 9 x 2-inch baking dish with foil; set aside.
3. Combine ground beef, egg, bread crumbs, oregano, and basil in medium-size bowl; season with salt and pepper. Using your hands, mix until well blended.
4. Turn mixture out onto 15-inch-long sheet of foil and shape into 9-inch square.
5. Layer Provolone slices over meat loaf, leaving 1-inch border around edges.
6. Using foil as a starter, roll the meat tightly, jelly-roll style, completely sealing cheese inside the meat loaf.
7. Transfer meat loaf to prepared baking dish, removing foil used for rolling, and bake 40 minutes.
8. Remove meat loaf from oven and set aside to rest about 5 minutes.
9. Cut meat loaf crosswise into ½-inch-thick slices and

divide among 4 dinner plates. Top with equal portions of tomato sauce, and garnish each serving with a sprig of parsley if desired.

Tomato Sauce

Small onion
1 clove garlic
2 tablespoons olive oil
25-ounce can crushed tomatoes
2 tablespoons chopped parsley
Salt and freshly ground pepper

1. Peel and chop enough onion to measure ½ cup.
2. Peel and mince enough garlic to measure 1 teaspoon.
3. Heat olive oil in medium-size heavy-gauge saucepan over medium-high heat. Add onion and garlic, and sauté, stirring occasionally, 2 to 3 minutes, or until softened and translucent.
4. Add tomatoes with their juice and bring to a boil.
5. Add parsley, and salt and pepper to taste; reduce heat and simmer gently, uncovered, 25 minutes.
6. Remove pan from heat, cover, and set aside until ready to serve.

Potato Pancakes

1½ pounds Russet potatoes
Small bunch scallions
2 eggs
½ cup milk
3 tablespoons all-purpose flour
Salt and freshly ground pepper
2 tablespoons vegetable oil, approximately

1. Fill medium-size bowl half full with cold water.
2. Peel potatoes, dropping each one into bowl of cold water as you finish peeling it.
3. Using food processor fitted with grating disk, or grater, grate potatoes. Return grated potatoes to medium-size bowl, add enough cold water to cover, and set aside.
4. Wash scallions and dry with paper towels. Trim ends and discard. Chop enough scallions to measure ½ cup.
5. Combine eggs, milk, scallions, flour, and salt and pepper to taste in large nonaluminum bowl and whisk until well blended.
6. Drain potatoes in colander and wring dry in kitchen towel. Add potatoes to egg mixture and stir to combine.
7. Heat 1 tablespoon oil in large cast-iron skillet or on griddle over medium-high heat until oil is hot but not smoking. Drop as many scant quarter-cupsful of batter as will fit comfortably in skillet or on griddle and cook pancakes about 2 minutes per side, or until golden.
8. Using metal spatula, transfer pancakes to heatproof platter, cover loosely with foil, and keep warm on stove top until ready to serve.
9. Stir remaining batter to recombine and repeat process, adding more oil if necessary.
10. If desired, warm pancakes in 200-degree oven for 5 minutes before serving.

Dorothee Polson

F or Dorothee Polson, home cooking means being able to adapt meals to the maturing palates of growing children. "When my three children were small," she says, "I found they favored only the simplest, blandest dishes. But as they grew up, I was gradually able to introduce more complicated meals with more complex flavors." Today her children have a keen appreciation for a wide range of foods, and Dorothee Polson can be as experimental as she likes in the kitchen. Nevertheless, she still has a fondness for simple foods, simply presented, and has created her three menus accordingly.

Menu 1 offers a variation on a standard frittata, or Italian open-faced omelet: The eggs are baked in the oven rather than cooked on top of the stove. A colorful sauté of red, green, and yellow peppers and a refreshing grated carrot salad are served with the frittata.

Menus 2 and 3 present dishes purely American in character. The Sloppy Joe sandwiches of Menu 2 are a popular skillet dish that originated in this country about twenty-five years ago. No one knows who Joe was, but the sandwiches are indeed messy and are best eaten with a knife and fork.

The Menu 3 entrée features cut-up turkey wings in a peppery sauce. The wings are accompanied by a fresh corn salad dotted with olives and scallions and sourdough rolls with herbed butter.

For a festive brunch or light supper, serve wedges of cheese-, sausage-, and potato-filled frittata with sautéed pepper strips and grated carrots mounded on lettuce leaves. Tomato juice is a fitting beverage.

Vegetable and Sausage Frittata
Three-Pepper Sauté
Carrot Salad

This baked frittata contains various savory ingredients including fresh Italian pork sausages. These sausages are sold either as one continuous length or as links; they can be sweet or hot and spicy. For this family meal, the sweet, mild type would be a better choice.

SHOPPING LIST AND STAPLES

4 sweet or hot Italian sausages (about ¾ pound total weight)
4 medium-size baking potatoes (about 1¾ pounds total weight)
2 medium-size onions (about 1 pound total weight)
3 or 4 large carrots (about 1 pound total weight)
1 each medium-size red, yellow, and green bell pepper (about 1¼ pounds total weight), or any combination
½ pint cherry tomatoes (optional)
1 head Boston lettuce
2 cloves garlic
Small bunch each fresh parsley and chives
Small bunch fresh marjoram, or 1 to 2 teaspoons dried
6 large eggs
1 stick plus 2 tablespoons unsalted butter
¼ pound Swiss cheese
½ cup olive oil, approximately
1 tablespoon red wine vinegar, approximately
Salt and freshly ground pepper

UTENSILS

2 medium-size heatproof skillets
Broiler pan
Wire rack
Medium-size bowl
Measuring cups and spoons
Chef's knife
Paring knife
Wooden spoon
Metal spatula
Whisk
Vegetable brush
Grater

START-TO-FINISH STEPS

Thirty minutes ahead: Set out eggs to come to room temperature for frittata recipe.

1. Wash parsley, chives, and marjoram if using, and dry with paper towels. Trim stem ends from parsley and marjoram, and discard. Set aside 4 sprigs parsley for garnish if desired, and mince enough parsley to measure 2 tablespoons for frittata recipe. Snip enough chives to measure 1 tablespoon for frittata recipe. Set aside 4 sprigs marjoram for garnish if desired, and mince enough marjoram to measure 1 tablespoon for salad recipe. Reserve remaining herbs for another use. Peel onions. Thinly slice each onion crosswise for frittata and peppers recipes; set aside.
2. Follow frittata recipe steps 1 through 9.
3. While frittata is baking, follow salad recipe steps 1 through 4.
4. Follow peppers recipe steps 1 through 4.
5. Just before peppers are done, follow frittata recipe step 10, and step 11 if desired.
6. Follow peppers recipe step 5, frittata recipe step 12, and serve with salad.

RECIPES

Vegetable and Sausage Frittata

1 stick unsalted butter
4 medium-size baking potatoes (about 1¾ pounds total weight)
Medium-size onion, peeled and thinly sliced
Salt and freshly ground pepper
4 sweet or hot Italian sausages (about ¾ pound total weight)
¼ pound Swiss cheese
6 large eggs, at room temperature
1 tablespoon freshly snipped chives
2 tablespoons minced parsley, plus 4 sprigs for garnish (optional)
2 cherry tomatoes for garnish (optional)

1. Preheat oven to 450 degrees.
2. Place butter in medium-size heatproof skillet and place skillet in oven to melt butter.
3. Meanwhile, scrub potatoes under cold running water with vegetable brush. Using chef's knife, cut potatoes crosswise into thin slices.
4. Remove skillet from oven and tilt and rotate pan to coat bottom evenly with butter. Arrange even layers of potato and onion slices in skillet, and sprinkle each layer with salt and freshly ground pepper to taste. Return skillet to oven

and cook potatoes and onion 10 minutes.

5. Meanwhile, cut uncooked sausages crosswise into ⅓-inch-thick slices. If sausage is soft, reshape with fingers. Arrange sausage slices in single layer on wire rack set in broiler pan and, with oven at 450 degrees, broil 4 inches from heating element 5 minutes, or just until excess fat is released.

6. Meanwhile, using grater, shred Swiss cheese; set aside.

7. Remove sausage from broiler; set aside.

8. In medium-size bowl, whisk eggs just until blended. Stir in chives and minced parsley.

9. Remove skillet from oven. Pour egg mixture over potatoes and onion, and, working quickly, arrange sausage slices in even layer over eggs. Top with shredded cheese and bake another 35 to 45 minutes, or until cheese is melted and golden and edges are browned.

10. Wash and dry cherry tomatoes, if using; set aside.

11. For a browner frittata, turn on broiler and place skillet in broiler 1 to 2 minutes, watching to avoid burning.

12. Cut fritatta into wedges and divide among 4 dinner plates. Garnish each plate with 1 cherry tomato half and a sprig of parsley, if desired.

Three-Pepper Sauté

1 each medium-size red, yellow, and green bell pepper (about 1¼ pounds total weight), or any combination
2 cloves garlic
2 tablespoons unsalted butter
2 tablespoons olive oil
Medium-size onion, peeled and thinly sliced
Salt and freshly ground pepper

1. Wash and dry peppers. Halve, core, and seed peppers. Cut lengthwise into 1½-inch-wide strips.

2. Peel and mince garlic; set aside.

3. Heat butter and olive oil in medium-size skillet over medium heat. When hot, add garlic and onion, and sauté about 1 minute, or just until garlic is cooked through.

4. Add pepper strips, season with salt and pepper to taste, and sauté, stirring occasionally, about 10 minutes, or just until peppers are crisp-tender but not overcooked.

5. Divide pepper sauté among 4 dinner plates and serve.

Carrot Salad

3 to 4 large carrots (about 1 pound total weight)
4 to 6 tablespoons olive oil
2 to 3 teaspoons red wine vinegar
1 tablespoon minced fresh marjoram, or 1 to 2 teaspoons dried, plus 4 sprigs for garnish (optional)
Salt and freshly ground pepper
1 head Boston lettuce

1. Peel and trim carrots. Using grater, grate enough carrots to measure 5 cups and turn into medium-size bowl.

2. Add oil, vinegar, minced marjoram, and salt and pepper to taste to carrots, and toss to combine; set aside.

3. Wash lettuce and dry with paper towels. Remove and discard any bruised or discolored leaves. Line 4 salad plates with lettuce; reserve remainder for another use.

4. Divide carrot salad among lettuce-lined plates and garnish each serving with a sprig of marjoram, if desired; set aside until ready to serve.

ADDED TOUCH

Because the bread is coarsely torn for this rich pudding, the dessert has a custard-like texture.

Bread Pudding with Citrus Sauce

Pudding:
¼ loaf stale white bread, preferably French or Italian, or enough to yield about 2 cups small pieces
2 cups half-and-half, or 1 cup milk and 1 cup heavy cream
4 eggs, at room temperature
1 tablespoon unsalted butter
½ cup pecan or almond pieces
½ cup firmly packed dark brown sugar
2 teaspoons vanilla extract
½ cup dark or golden raisins
½ cup unsweetened flaked coconut
1 teaspoon each cinnamon and freshly grated nutmeg

Sauce:
1 stick unsalted butter, at room temperature
1⅔ cups confectioners' sugar, sifted
1 egg
½ cup freshly squeezed orange juice, other citrus fruit juice, or orange-flavored liqueur

1. Preheat oven to 400 degrees.

2. Tear bread into small pieces (do not crumble) and place in large bowl. Add half-and-half or milk and cream and stir until bread has absorbed all liquid.

3. Break eggs into small bowl and beat lightly just until blended. Add eggs to bread mixture and stir until blended.

4. Melt 1 tablespoon butter in small nonaluminum saucepan or butter warmer over low heat.

5. Meanwhile, coarsely chop nuts; set aside.

6. Butter 9-inch round baking pan; set aside.

7. Add melted butter, nuts, brown sugar, and remaining pudding ingredients to bread mixture and stir to combine.

8. Turn mixture into prepared pan and bake 1 hour, or until set.

9. For sauce, cream together butter and confectioners' sugar in medium-size bowl, stirring until light and fluffy.

10. Turn mixture into small saucepan and heat over medium heat 1 to 2 minutes, or until warmed but not melted.

11. Meanwhile, separate egg, placing yolk in measuring cup and reserving white for another use.

12. Remove pan from heat. Add yolk and stir until blended. Stirring continuously, slowly add juice or liqueur and stir until totally incorporated; set sauce aside until ready to serve. Sauce will thicken as it cools.

13. Remove pudding from oven and set aside to cool at least 1 hour.

14. Cut pudding into wedges and divide among 4 dessert plates. Top each serving with some sauce and serve.

Sloppy Joes
Oven Fries
Easy Chocolate Milk Shakes

Overstuffed Sloppy Joe sandwiches, oven fries, and frothy milk shakes will delight even those hard-to-please eaters.

Hungry youngsters will love these hearty sandwiches of meat in tomato sauce spooned over split buns. You can turn Sloppy Joes into their south-of-the-border cousins —Sloppy Josés—by using diced green chilies instead of the cucumber as a topping.

For a richer milk shake, blend the milk and chocolate syrup with one or two scoops of slightly softened high-quality vanilla or chocolate ice cream, but don't overmix.

SHOPPING LIST AND STAPLES

1½ pounds very lean ground beef
3 large baking potatoes (about 1¾ pounds total weight)
Medium-size onion
4 medium-size white mushrooms (optional)
Small cucumber, or 4-ounce can diced green chilies (optional)
Small tomato (optional)
½ pint cherry tomatoes (optional)
1 quart milk
4 tablespoons unsalted butter, approximately

8-ounce can tomato sauce
6-ounce can tomato paste
2 tablespoons vegetable oil
2 tablespoons whole-grain mustard
8-ounce jar midget gherkins (optional)
3½-ounce can pitted black olives (optional)
¼ cup chocolate syrup
4 soft bakery buns or sesame rolls
Salt and freshly ground pepper

UTENSILS

Blender
Large heavy-gauge skillet
13 x 9 x 2-inch baking dish
3 small bowls
Strainer
Measuring cups and spoons
Serrated bread knife
Chef's knife
Paring knife

Wooden spoon
Metal spatula
Vegetable brush

START-TO-FINISH STEPS

1. Follow oven fries recipe steps 1 through 4.
2. While potatoes are baking, follow Sloppy Joes recipe steps 1 through 3.
3. Follow oven fries recipe step 5.
4. While potatoes are baking, follow Sloppy Joes recipe steps 4 through 6.
5. Follow milk shakes recipe steps 1 through 3.
6. Follow Sloppy Joes recipe step 7, oven fries recipe step 6, and serve with milk shakes.

RECIPES

Sloppy Joes

Toppings (optional):
Small tomato
Small cucumber, or ½ cup diced green chilies
4 medium-size white mushrooms

Garnishes (optional):
4 cherry tomatoes
4 pitted black olives
4 midget gherkins

Filling:
Medium-size onion
2 tablespoons vegetable oil
1½ pounds very lean ground beef
8-ounce can tomato sauce
6-ounce can tomato paste
2 tablespoons whole-grain mustard
Freshly ground pepper
4 soft bakery buns or sesame rolls

1. Prepare toppings, if using: Wash and dry tomato; core and dice. Peel and dice cucumber, if using. Wipe mushrooms clean with damp paper towels; cut into thin slices. If using chilies, turn into strainer and rinse. Drain and dry. Place tomato, mushrooms, and cucumber or chilies in separate bowls, cover with plastic wrap, and refrigerate until ready to serve.
2. Prepare garnishes, if using: Wash and dry cherry toma-

toes. Drain olives and gherkins. Set aside.
3. For filling, peel and finely chop enough onion to measure 1 cup; set aside.
4. Heat oil in large heavy-gauge skillet over medium-high heat. Add meat, stirring with wooden spoon to break up lumps; cook 2 to 3 minutes, or until meat starts to brown.
5. Drain off fat and excess oil from skillet. Add onion, tomato sauce, tomato paste, mustard, and pepper to taste, and stir to combine. Simmer, uncovered, stirring occasionally, 10 minutes.
6. Meanwhile, split buns in half, wrap in foil, and place in preheated oven to warm.
7. When ready to serve, place warm buns on 4 dinner plates and top one half of each with equal portion of filling. Sprinkle each serving with desired topping(s), and garnish with a tomato, olive, and gherkin, if desired.

Oven Fries

4 tablespoons unsalted butter, approximately
3 large baking potatoes (about 1¾ pounds total weight)
Salt and freshly ground pepper

1. Preheat oven to 400 degrees.
2. Place 3 tablespoons butter in 13 x 9 x 2-inch baking dish and place dish in oven to melt butter.
3. With vegetable brush, scrub potatoes under cold running water. Do not peel. Using chef's knife, cut potatoes lengthwise into ½- to ¾-inch-thick slices, then cut slices into ½-inch-wide strips.
4. Remove dish from oven and, working quickly, arrange potatoes in a single layer. Sprinkle lightly with salt and generously with freshly ground pepper, return to oven, and bake 30 minutes.
5. Using metal spatula, turn potatoes over, so tops are in melted butter, adding more butter if necessary. Return potatoes to oven and bake another 20 to 30 minutes, or until potatoes are tender and golden.
6. Divide potatoes among 4 dinner plates and serve.

Easy Chocolate Milk Shakes

¼ cup chocolate syrup
4 cups cold milk

1. Just before serving, combine chocolate syrup and ¼ cup milk in blender and mix until blended.
2. Add remaining milk and blend just until frothy.
3. Divide among 4 cups or glasses and serve cold.

Tangy Turkey Wings
Corn Salad
Sourdough Rolls with Herbed Butter

Create a family picnic indoors or out with spicy turkey wings, corn salad, and herb-buttered sourdough rolls.

The succulent turkey wings require nearly an hour to bake, so prepare them first. If you prefer a milder flavor, decrease the amount of red pepper sauce to taste.

Sourdough bread owes its characteristic—and pleasant —tang to the sour yeast starter used for leavening. Most supermarkets stock sourdough rolls or breads, which are a perfect foil for the fresh-herb butter. If sourdough baked goods are not available, use French or Italian rolls.

SHOPPING LIST AND STAPLES

4 large turkey wings (about 3 pounds total weight)
4 large ears fresh corn on the cob, or two 10-ounce packages frozen corn kernels
1 each small red and green bell pepper
Small bunch scallions
1 clove garlic
Small bunch fresh savory, or 1 tablespoon dried
Small bunch fresh thyme, or 1 tablespoon dried
1 stick plus 6 tablespoons unsalted butter
1 tablespoon hot pepper sauce, approximately
4¾-ounce jar pimiento-stuffed green olives
4 sourdough rolls
Salt and freshly ground pepper

UTENSILS

Stockpot or large saucepan
Small saucepan
13 x 9 x 2-inch baking dish
Small bowl
Colander
Measuring cups and spoons
Cleaver (optional)
Serrated bread knife
Chef's knife
Paring knife
Wooden spoon
Metal tongs
Basting brush
Vegetable brush

START-TO-FINISH STEPS

One hour ahead: Set out butter to come to room temperature for rolls recipe.

1. Follow turkey wings recipe steps 1 through 6.
2. While wings are baking, follow corn salad recipe steps 1 through 5.
3. Follow turkey wings recipe step 7.
4. While wings are baking, follow corn salad recipe steps 6 and 7, and rolls recipe steps 1 through 5.
5. Follow turkey wings recipe step 8, rolls recipe step 6, and serve with corn salad.

RECIPES

Tangy Turkey Wings

Small red bell pepper
Small green bell pepper
4 large turkey wings (about 3 pounds total weight)
6 tablespoons unsalted butter
1 tablespoon hot pepper sauce, approximately
Salt and freshly ground pepper

1. Preheat oven to 450 degrees.
2. Wash peppers and dry with paper towels. Halve, core, and seed peppers. Finely dice one half of each pepper; set aside. Reserve remaining halves for another use.
3. Wash turkey wings under cold running water and dry with paper towels. Using cleaver or sharp chef's knife, cut each wing through joints into 3 pieces. Reserve bony tip sections for stock and arrange remaining 8 pieces in single layer in 13 x 9 x 2-inch baking dish; set aside.
4. Melt butter in small saucepan over low heat, watching carefully to prevent burning.
5. Add diced bell peppers, hot pepper sauce, and salt and pepper to taste, and stir to combine. Remove pan from heat and keep sauce warm on stovetop.
6. With basting brush, baste wings with some of the sauce and bake 20 minutes.
7. Remove baking dish from oven and, working quickly, turn wings and baste again. Return wings to oven and bake another 20 to 25 minutes, or until juices run clear when wings are pierced with tip of knife.
8. Remove baking dish from oven. Pour remaining sauce over wings and serve hot.

Corn Salad

4 large ears fresh corn on the cob, or two 10-ounce
   packages frozen corn kernels
4¾-ounce jar pimiento-stuffed green olives

Small bunch scallions
Salt
Freshly ground pepper

1. If using fresh corn, fill stockpot or large saucepan two-thirds full with cold water and bring to a boil over high heat.
2. While water is heating, remove husks and silk from corn and discard. With dry vegetable brush, brush ears free of any strands of silk. Drop ears into boiling water, making sure they can move freely, and boil 4 to 6 minutes, depending on size of ears, or until tender but still slightly crisp. If using frozen corn, cook according to package directions.
3. Meanwhile, drain olives and coarsely chop enough to measure 2 tablespoons; reserve remaining olives for another use.
4. Using tongs, transfer fresh corn to colander or turn corn kernels into colander and refresh under cold running water.
5. Wash scallions and dry with paper towels. Trim ends and discard. Chop enough scallions to measure ¾ cup; set aside.
6. When corn on the cob is cool enough to handle, remove kernels: Holding 1 ear of corn upright, press base against work surface and, with chef's knife, cut off kernels by pressing blade against cob and slicing downward. Turn corn and repeat process until all kernels are removed. Repeat process for remaining ears. You should have about 2½ cups kernels.

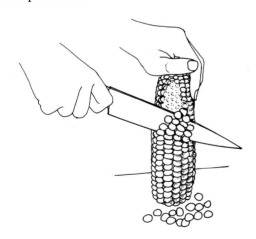

7. Combine corn kernels, chopped scallions, olives, and salt and pepper to taste in serving dish and toss to com-

bine. Taste and adjust seasoning; set aside until ready to serve.

Sourdough Rolls with Herbed Butter

Small bunch fresh savory, or 1 tablespoon dried
Small bunch fresh thyme, or 1 tablespoon dried
1 clove garlic
1 stick unsalted butter, at room temperature
4 sourdough rolls

1. If using fresh savory and thyme, wash and dry. Trim stem ends and discard. Chop enough savory and thyme to measure 2 tablespoons each; set aside. Reserve remainder for another use.
2. Peel and mince enough garlic to measure 1 teaspoon.
3. Combine butter, garlic, and herbs in small bowl and stir until well blended.
4. With bread knife, cut rolls crosswise into 4 slices, cutting only to within ¼ inch of bottom; do *not* cut all the way through. Spread cut sides of each slice with herb butter. If there is any butter remaining, spread across top of each roll.
5. Wrap each roll in foil and place in preheated oven to warm for 5 minutes.
6. When warm, unwrap rolls, place in napkin-lined basket, and serve.

ADDED TOUCH

Spoon this rich, creamy dessert into individual bowls and serve with fruit or cookies, if desired.

Chocolate Ricotta

Two 1-ounce squares semisweet chocolate
Whole nutmeg
15-ounce container ricotta cheese
½ cup confectioners' sugar

1. Using fine side of grater, grate chocolate over sheet of waxed paper; set aside.
2. Without washing grater, grate about 1½ teaspoons nutmeg over separate sheet of waxed paper.
3. Combine ricotta cheese, sugar, half of the chocolate, and nutmeg to taste in small serving bowl and stir until blended. Sprinkle remaining chocolate over top, cover with plastic wrap, and refrigerate until ready to serve.

Acknowledgments

Special thanks are due to Carol Baer of the Popover Cafe in New York City.

The Editors would like to thank the following for their courtesy in lending items for photography: *Cover:* plate—Marimekko. *Frontispiece:* dishes—Mood Indigo; plastic glass—Fitz & Floyd; tablecloth—Marimekko. *Pages 18–19:* plates—Oleksa Collection; board—Pottery Barn; tablecloth—Conran's. *Page 22:* plate—Oleksa Collection. *Page 25:* bowl—Pan American Phoenix; servers—The Lauffer Co. *Pages 28–29:* tablecloth—Laura Ashley. *Page 32:* dishes, salt and pepper shakers—Fitz & Floyd. *Page 34:* plates—Franciscan Ceramics, Inc.; basket—Be Seated; silver—Gorham; glasses—Conran's. *Pages 36–37:* plates, mugs—MacKenzie-Childs, Ltd.; flatware—Gorham; baking dish—Wolfman-Gold & Good Co. *Pages* 40–41: platters, wooden board—Pottery Barn; tablecloth—Conran's. *Page 43:* glasses, underplates, napkins—Frank McIntosh at Henri Bendel; plates—Oleksa Collection. *Pages 46–47:* plates—Conran's; napkin, glasses—Pottery Barn; tiles—Nemo Tile; flatware—Gorham. *Page 50:* mat—Susskind Collection. *Page 52:* tablecloth—Conran's; fork—The Lauffer Co.; mug, plate—Marimekko courtesy of Pottery Barn; basket, napkin—Pottery Barn. *Pages 54–55:* glass, tablecloth—Conran's; plate—Pottery Barn. *Page 58:* platters—Dan Bleier courtesy of Creative Resources. *Page 61:* dishes, glass, napkin—Creative Resources. *Pages 64–65:* tiles—Country Floors, Inc.; dishes, glasses, pitcher—Pottery Barn. *Pages 68–69:* platters—Deruta of Italy. *Page 71:* plate—Mad Monk; flatware—Gorham; baking dish—Wolfman-Gold & Good Co. *Pages 74–75:* tiles—Nemo Tile; bowl—Mad Monk. *Page 78:* tablecloth, plates, glass—Pan American Phoenix. *Page 81:* mat—Folklorica; black bowl—Mad Monk. *Pages 84–85:* dishes—Mad Monk; basket—Be Seated. *Page 88:* Dan Bleier. *Page 90:* fork—Gorham. *Pages 92–93:* dishes, napkin—Pottery Barn; forks—Gorham; tablecloth—Conran's. *Page 96:* plates—Pottery Barn; glasses, napkins—Conran's. *Page 98:* plates, napkin, basket, glasses—Conran's; glass carrier, glass casserole—Pottery Barn. *Kitchen equipment courtesy of:* White-Westinghouse, Commercial Aluminum Cookware Co., Robot-Coupe, Caloric, Kitchen-Aid, J.A. Henckels Zwillingswerk, Inc., and Schwabel Corp. Microwave oven compliments of Litton Microwave Cooking Products.
Illustrations by Ray Skibinski
Production by Giga Communications

Index